Women Explorers

Sue Hendrickson
Explorer of Land and Sea

Women Explorers

Annie Montague Alexander
Naturalist and Fossil Hunter

Gertrude Bell
Explorer of the Middle East

Alexandra David-Néel
Explorer at the Roof of the World

Sylvia Earle
Deep-Sea Explorer

Sue Hendrickson
Explorer of Land and Sea

Mary Kingsley
Explorer of the Congo

Women
Explorers

Sue Hendrickson
Explorer of Land and Sea

Ann Gaines

Introduction: Milbry Polk,
author of *Women of Discovery*

CHELSEA HOUSE
P U B L I S H E R S
A Haights Cross Communications ◆ Company
Philadelphia

CHELSEA HOUSE PUBLISHERS
VP, NEW PRODUCT DEVELOPMENT Sally Cheney
DIRECTOR OF PRODUCTION Kim Shinners
CREATIVE MANAGER Takeshi Takahashi
MANUFACTURING MANAGER Diann Grasse

Staff for SUE HENDRICKSON
ASSOCIATE EDITOR Kate Sullivan
PHOTO EDITOR Sarah Bloom
PRODUCTION EDITOR Megan Emery
SERIES & COVER DESIGNER Terry Mallon
LAYOUT 21st Century Publishing and Communications, Inc.

A Haights Cross Communications ✦ Company

http://www.chelseahouse.com

First Printing

9 8 7 6 5 4 3 2 1

Library of Congress Cataloging-in-Publication Data

Gaines, Ann.
    Sue Hendrickson : explorer on land and sea/by Ann Gaines.
        v. cm.—(Women explorers)
    Includes bibliographical references (p.) and index.
    Contents: A hard time fitting in, 1949–1965—Diving, 1966–1973—
    Marine archeology, 1973–1983—Fossils, 1983–1985—Paleontology—
    Sue—Hendrickson after Sue, 1992-2003—Hendrickson's influence.
        ISBN 0-7910-7713-6
    1. Hendrickson, Sue, 1949– Juvenile literature. 2. Paleontologists—
    United States—Biography. [1. Hendrickson, Sue, 1949– 2. Paleontolo-
    gists. 3. Women—Biography.] I. Title. II. Series.
    QE707.H46G35 2004
    560'.92—dc22
                                                            2003026138

Table of Contents

Introduction

By Milbry Polk

Curiosity is one of the most compelling forces of human
life. Our desire to understand who and what and where
we are drives us restlessly to explore and to comprehend
what we see. Every historical era is known by the individuals
who sought to expand our boundaries of time and space
and knowledge. People such as Alexander the Great, Ibn
Battuta, Marco Polo, Ferdinand Magellan, Hernando de
Soto, Meriwether Lewis, William Clark, Charles Darwin,
Sir Richard Burton, Roald Amundsen, Jacques Cousteau,
Edmund Hillary, Tenzing Norgay, Thor Hyerdahl, and Neil
Armstrong are men whose discoveries changed our worldview. They were explorers, leaders into the unknown. This
series is about a handful of individuals who have been left
out of the history books but whose feats loom large, whose
discoveries changed the way we look at the world. They are
women explorers.

WHAT MAKES SOMEONE AN EXPLORER?
The desire to know what lies beyond the next hill—the desire
to explore—is one of the most powerful of human impulses.
This drive makes us unique among the species with which
we share our earth. Curiosity helped to impel our remote
ancestors out of Africa. It is what spread them in waves
throughout the world where they settled; curiosity helped
them adapt to the many environments they encountered.

Myths of all cultures include the memories of early
explorations. These myths were the means by which people
explained to themselves and taught their children about life,

about the world around them, and about death. Myths helped people make sense of the inexplicable forces of nature and the strangeness of new lands and peoples. The few myths and legends that have come down to us are the stories of early exploration.

What makes someone an explorer? The qualities required are not unique. We are born explorers. Every child, even in the crib, is reaching out, trying to understand, to take the measure of its own body, then its immediate surroundings, and we continue as we go through life to grasp ever-widening circles of experience and reality. As we grow up, we often lose the excitement of the child, the characteristic that supposedly gave Albert Einstein his ability to see the universe in a new way. What typifies the explorer is not losing this wonderful childlike curiosity. He or she still reaches out. Explorers are open minded—able to look at and accept what they see, rather than to fall back upon preconceived notions. Explorers are courageous, not just in facing physical danger, but also in having the courage to confront failure, ridicule, and laughter, and yet to keep on going. Above all, explorers have the ability to communicate. All insights, observations, and discoveries mean nothing to the wider community if they are not documented and shared. An explorer goes out into the world at some personal risk and discovers something of value and then shares that knowledge with his or her community. Explorers are leaders who look at the world in new ways and in doing so make breakthroughs that enrich all of our lives.

WOMEN EXPLORERS

Women, like men, have always been explorers. Typically in a "hunter-gatherer" society the men hunted animals while the women ventured far from the camps in search of other foods. Though their tasks were different, both were explorers. And, since such societies were almost constantly on the move, women were there for each voyage of discovery. But over time, as cultural groups became more settled, ideas began to change about the role of women in society. Women came to be restricted to the house, the shared courtyard, or the village and began to wear clothing that set them apart. By the time of the Middle Ages often the only way women in the Western world could travel was by going on pilgrimage. The trek to visit holy sites offered women one of the few opportunities to see new places, hear new languages, and meet different people. In fact, the first autobiography in the English language was written by a pilgrim, Margery Kempe (1373–1440), about her journeys throughout Europe and to the Holy Land.

Over time, women became formally excluded from exploration. Of course, some women did manage to find a way around the obstacles. Those who did venture forth went alone or in disguise and often needed men to help them. But their stories were not recorded in official histories; to find their stories one has to dig deep.

About three hundred years ago, the western worldview changed. Beginning in the 1700s, the scientific revolution began to change life for everyone in Europe. Men as well as women were swept up in the excitement to classify and understand every aspect of life on earth. Legions of people went to every corner of the world to see and record what was there. The spirit of adventure began to find new means of expression. New modes of transportation made movement around the world easier and new technologies made recording events and communication less expensive and more vivid.

The findings of these explorers were fascinating to the people back home. Wealthy individuals collected many of the strange insects, botanical specimens, native art, rocks, and other findings, brought back by the explorers into personal collections called Cabinets of Curiosities. These Cabinets of

Curiosities are the forerunners of our modern museums. The desire to collect the unusual financed expeditions, which in turn fostered public interest in exploration. The creation and spread of scientific and popular magazines with stories about expeditions and discoveries enabled the public to learn about the world. By the 1800s, explorers had the status of popular heroes in the public eye. The lure of the unknown gripped society.

Unlike men, women did not have support of institutions such as universities, museums, scientific societies, governments, and the military that sponsored and financed exploration. Until well into the twentieth century, many of these institutions barred women from participation, membership, and especially leadership. Women were thought capable of gathering things such as flowers or rocks for subjects to paint and draw, but men were the ones who studied them, named them, and published books about them. Most women, if they had any specialized education at all, gained it through private tutors. Men went to the university. Men formed and joined scientific societies and the exploring clubs. Men ran the governments, the military, and the press, and archived the collections. Universities and other cultural institutions were open only to the membership of men. Women were generally excluded from them. When these institutions sponsored exploration, they sponsored men. Women not only had to overcome mountains in the wild but also institutions at home.

In the 1800s women were not usually trained or taught academics. Instead, they learned sewing, music, and how to behave as a lady. A woman who managed to learn to write overcame great obstacles. Few managed to do it, but the same spirit that made women into explorers animated their minds in other ways. A few women learned to record what they were doing sufficiently well that at least some of their works have become classics of description and adventure.

Because of them, we know the little we do know about their lives and actions. As the nineteenth century progressed, more and more women were going out collecting, recording, and writing about faraway places. By the late 1800s more women were educated and those who traveled often wrote accounts of their journeys. So, now, in the twenty-first century, we are just beginning to learn about the unknown side of exploration—the women's story—from the accounts that lay buried in our archives.

And what a story it is. For example, one of the first modern women explorers was Maria Sybila Merian, who sailed to Surinam in 1699 at the age of 52. Not content to view the strange flora and fauna that were arriving back in Europe to fill the Cabinets of Curiosity, she wanted to collect and paint insects and animals in their native habitat.

Western women also faced societal obstacles; they generally could not go anywhere without a chaperon. So for a would-be woman explorer, a night in the wild spent in the company of a man who was not a close relative or her husband was unthinkable. And then there were the unsuitable clothes. In many parts of the early modern world it was punishable by death (as it was in Spain in the 1600s) or imprisonment (as it was in America well into the late 1800s) for women to appear in public wearing pants.

The heavy, layered dresses and tight corsets thought necessary for women made traveling very cumbersome. For example, when the Alps began to be climbed by explorers in the 1800s, a few women were caught up in the mania. The first two women to summit the Matterhorn climbed in skirts and corsets. The third woman, an American professor of Latin, Annie Smith Peck (1850–1935), realized the absurdity of leaping crevasses, climbing ice walls, and enduring the winds in a skirt. So, she wore pants. This created such a sensation in 1895 that the Singer Sewing

Machine Company photographed her and included a card with her in climbing gear with every machine it sold.

THE WOMEN EXPLORERS SERIES

When asked why he wanted to climb Mount Everest, George Mallory famously replied, "Because it's there." Perhaps another explorer would answer the same question, "Because I don't know what is there and I want to find out."

Although we all have curiosity, what separates explorers is their willingness to take their curiosity further. Despite the odds, a lack of money, and every imaginable difficulty, they still find a way to go. They do so because they are passionate about life and their passion carries them over the barriers. As you will discover, the women profiled in this series shared that passion. Their passion gave them the strength to face what would seem to be insurmountable odds to most of us. To read their stories is more than learning about the adventure, it is a guide to discovering our own passions. The women in this series, Mary Kingsley, Gertrude Bell, Alexandra David-Néel, Annie Montague Alexander, Sue Hendrickson, and Sylvia Earle, all join the pantheon of explorers, the heroes of our age.

These six women have been chosen because their interests range from geographical to cultural exploration; from traversing the highest mountains to diving to the depths of the oceans; from learning about life far back in time to looking forward into the future. These women are extraordinary leaders and thinkers. They are all individuals who have braved the unknown and challenged the traditional women's roles. Their discoveries have had remarkable and profound effects on what we know about the world. To be an explorer one does not have to be wealthy or have multiple degrees. To be an explorer one must have the desire from within and focus on the destination: the unknown.

Mary Kingsley (1862–1900) was the daughter of an English Victorian gentleman-explorer who believed women did not need to be educated. Mary was kept at home and only tutored in German to translate articles her father wanted to read. But while he was away, she went into his library and educated herself by reading his books. She never married and followed the custom of her day for unmarried women by staying home with her parents. When her parents died she found herself alone—and suddenly free. She purchased a ticket to the Canary Islands with her inheritance. Once there, she learned about the Congo, then considered by the Europeans to be a terrifying place. When Kingsley decided to go to the Congo, she was warned that all she would find would be festering swamplands laced with deadly diseases and cannibals. Kingsley viewed that warning as a challenge. Having used up all her money on the ticket, she outfitted herself as a trader. She returned to the Congo, and in a wooden canoe she plied the tributaries of the Congo River, trading goods with the natives and collecting fish for the British Museum. She learned the languages of the interior and befriended the local tribes. She became an expert on their rich belief systems, which were completely unknown in Europe. Like many explorers, Mary Kingsley's knowledge bridged separate worlds, helping each understand and appreciate the other.

Gertrude Bell (1868–1926) was the daughter of a wealthy English industrialist. She had tremendous ambition, which she used to convince her parents to give her an education at a time when, for a woman, education was considered secondary to a good marriage. As a result of her intelligence and determination, she won one of the few coveted spots for women at Oxford University. After college, she did not know what to do. Girls of her class usually waited at home for a proposal of marriage. But after Bell returned home, she received an invitation from her uncle to visit Persia (modern-day Iran). Quickly, she set about learning Persian. Later she learned Arabic and begin her own archeological trips into the Syrian deserts.

When World War I broke out, Bell was in the Middle East. Her ability to speak the language, as well as her knowledge of the local tribes and the deserts from her archeological work, caused the British to appoint her to one of the most important jobs in the Desert War, that of Oriental Secretary. The Oriental Secretary was the officer of the embassy who was expected to know about and deal with local affairs, roughly what we call a political officer in an embassy. Bell played a major role in crafting the division of the Middle East into the countries we know today. She also founded the museum in Iraq.

Alexandra David-Néel (1868–1969) was performing in the Paris Opera when she married a banker. As she now had some financial freedom, she decided to act on her lifelong dream to travel to the East. Soon after she married, she sailed alone for India. She assured her husband she be gone only about 18 months; it would be 24 years before she would return home. Upon arriving in India she became intrigued with the Buddhist religion. She felt in order to understand Buddhism, she had first to master Tibetan, the language in which many of the texts were written. In the course of doing so, she plunged so deeply into the culture that she became a Buddhist nun. After several years of study, David-Néel became determined to visit the home of the spiritual leader of the Tibetan Buddhists, the Dalai Lama, who resided in the Holy City of Lhasa, in Tibet. This was quite a challenge because all foreigners were forbidden from entering Lhasa. At the age of 55, she began a long and arduous winter trek across the Himalayas toward Tibet. She succeeded in becoming the first Western woman to visit Lhasa. After returning to France, David-Néel dedicated the rest of her long life to helping Westerners understand the beauty and complexity of Buddhist religion and culture through her many writings.

A wealthy and restless young woman, Annie Montague Alexander (1867–1950) decided to pursue her interests in science and nature rather than live the life of a socialite in San Francisco. She organized numerous expeditions throughout the American West to collect flora, fauna, and fossils. Concerned by the rapid changes occurring due to the growing population, Alexander envisaged a time, all too soon, when much of the natural world of the West would be gone due to urbanization and agricultural development. As a tribute to the land she loved, she decided to create the best natural history museum of the American West. She actually created two museums at the University of California, Berkeley, in which to house the thousands of specimens she had assembled. In the course of her exploration, she discovered new species, seventeen of which are named for her. Though little known, Alexander contributed much to our knowledge of American zoology and paleontology.

Two women in this series are still actively exploring. Sue Hendrickson dropped out of high school and made a living by collecting fish off the Florida Keys to sell to aquariums. An invitation to go on an underwater dive trip changed her life. She became passionate about diving, and soon found herself working with archeologists on wrecks. Hendrickson was often the lead diver, diving first to find out what was there. She realized she had a knack for seeing things others missed. On land, she became an amber collector of pieces of fossilized resin that contained insects and later became a dinosaur hunter. While on a fossil expedition in the Badlands of the Dakotas, Hendrickson discovered the largest *Tyrannosaurus rex* ever found. It has been named Sue in her honor. Depending on the time of year, she can be found diving in the sunken ancient port of Alexandria, Egypt, mapping Spanish wrecks off Cuba's coastline, or in the high, dry lands of ancient forests hunting for dinosaur bones.

Sylvia Earle began her exploration of the sea in the early days of scuba. Smitten with the undersea world, she earned degrees in biology and oceanography. She wanted more than to just study the sea; she wanted to live in the sea. In the early 1970s, Earle was eager to take part in a project in which humans lived in a module underwater for extended periods of time for the U.S. Navy. Unfortunately, when the project was about to begin, she was informed that because she was a woman, she could not go. Undaunted, Earle designed the next phase of the project exclusively for women. This project had far-reaching results. It proved to the U.S. military that women could live well in a confined environment and opened the door for women's entry into the space program.

Earle, ever reaching for new challenges, began designing and testing submersibles, which would allow a human to experience the underwater world more intimately than anything created up to that time. Approaching age 70, her goal is to explore the deepest, darkest place on earth: the 35,800-foot-deep Marianas Trench south of Guam, in the Pacific Ocean.

The experiences of these six women illustrate different paths, different experiences, and different situations, but each led to a similar fulfillment in exploration. All are explorers; all have given us the gift of understanding some aspect of our world. All offer tremendous opportunities to us. Each of us can learn from them and follow in their paths. They are trailblazers; but many trails remain unexplored. There is so much unknown about the world, so much that needs to be understood. For example, less than 5 percent of the ocean has been explored. Thousands of species of plants and animals wait to be discovered. We have not reached every place on earth, and of what we have seen, we often understand very little. Today, we are embarked on the greatest age of exploration. And we go armed with more knowledge than any of the explorers who have gone before us.

What these women teach us is that we need explorers to help us understand what is miraculous in the world around us. The goal for each of us is to find his or her own path and begin the journey.

1

"You Found Me!"

When explorer Sue Hendrickson awoke on August 12, 1990, she had no idea that she was about to make history. For the third summer in a row, she was working as a volunteer for the Black Hills Institute of Geological Research in the Badlands of South Dakota, taking part in a dinosaur dig.[1] The main work of the summer had been completed at the Ruth Mason Quarry, where, for 15 years, Pete Larson, head of the Institute, and a crew had been collecting hadrosaur—duck-billed dinosaur—bones. Now, as the summer waned, almost all of the Institute's crew members had packed their bags and gone home. Five people—Larson; Hendrickson; Terry Wentz (a preparator for the institute); Larson's son Matt; and Larson's nephew Jason—had yet to return to their regular lives. Instead, they remained behind to take care of one final matter: excavating a juvenile triceratops skull Matt had found on Sharkey Williams' ranch, located near the Mason quarry, in the north-central part of the state.

That morning, as always, they awoke early. Everybody expected to work without a break until darkness fell. Their plans went awry, however, when they discovered that not only did their truck have a flat tire but that the spare appeared low as well. When Larson announced that he needed to head into the nearby town of Faith to get both tires repaired, everyone except Hendrickson decided to tag along.

Although Sue Hendrickson was as tired as the rest of the crew, she stayed behind. She had something specific she wanted to do with the time to herself. For days, whenever she began to feel cramped from squatting to chip away at the stone in which the triceratops skull was trapped, she would rise to her feet and look across dusty plains and Badlands to a sandstone cliff on an adjoining ranch.

Because the Institute had been working in the area for years, she knew that the geologic formation was part of the Hell Creek Formation and dated from the late Cretaceous, the third and last period of the Mesozoic era, at the end of which—about 65 million years ago—the dinosaurs disappeared.

At the Ruth Mason Quarry in South Dakota, members of the Black Hills Institute's geological research team diligently collected hadrosaur bones in the summer of 1990. The Black Hills Institute, and its leader Peter Larson, would later become famous for another specimen they would excavate that summer—Sue, the most complete *T. rex* ever discovered.

Hendrickson was aware that Maurice Williams, brother of Sharkey, owned the land the cliff ran across. Williams had specifically invited the BHI crew to venture over to hunt for fossils on his property, too. His only stipulation had been that no one drive on his land. Hendrickson and the others had already covered some ground on his ranch, but not that particular area.

Confident that she would not be charged with trespassing, Hendrickson set off with her faithful golden retriever, Gypsy, to investigate the cliff that she had spotted two weeks earlier from across the valley. Fog—virtually unheard of in that part of the world in the heat of August—caused her to become disoriented, and after two hours Hendrickson realized she had walked in a complete circle. Luckily, by then the fog had begun to lift, and she set out once more to the cliff she felt calling to her. Finally they reached the base of the cliff. Using a tried-and-true technique she stumbled on as a small child (she had started her lifelong habit of searching for "treasure" by the time she was four years old), Hendrickson walked with her head down, looking at the ground.[2] She scanned the hard-packed, parched earth for loose bone fragments or teeth from the wall above.

Walking along, she suddenly spotted what she had been searching for: fossilized bone fragments, pieces measuring one or two inches long, which had fallen from the cliff above. Picking them up, she was excited to see that these bones were light in weight and riddled with holes, just like birds' bones. That honeycomb texture (the technical term is "camellate structure") is recognized by paleontologists as being characteristic of carnivorous dinosaurs' bones.[3] Stopping to look, she immediately knew where her fragments had come from: There, eight feet above her head, were three plate-sized, articulated vertebrae sticking out from the rock. The vertebrae's huge size made her heart pound even harder, because she knew that there was only one carnivore who lived in the area in the late Cretaceous who would have had such big bones: a *Tyrannosaurus rex.*[4]

The *T. rex* is one dinosaur that it seems virtually everyone knows something about. What relatively few people realize, however, is that knowledge of this fearsome beast is based on only a few skeletons. By 1990, in fact, only ten other *T. rex* specimens had been discovered. Most of them were extremely incomplete, with six lacking three-quarters of their bones.[5] Hendrickson knew well that any new *T. rex* discovery—"even two bones,"[6] as she says— would hold great significance for the scientific community.

When talking about her discovery, Hendrickson never downplays her own skill or tenacity, but she seems to mention most often her sense that this skeleton wanted to be found. Looking back on why she felt so drawn to that one spot, she reached a simple enough explanation: "[The *T. rex*] knew we were going to leave, so she got desperate."[7] Hendrickson likes to imagine that Sue—the name given to the skeleton in Hendrickson's honor—used her short arm and claws to puncture that truck tire in order to give Hendrickson the opportunity to find her. When Hendrickson finally saw Sue's skull, she laughed because she got a sense that Sue was grinning at her and gleefully shouting "You found me!"[8]

The impact of her find growing on her, Hendrickson raced back to the triceratops dig with Gypsy at her side. She was elated to find that Larson was back from his trip into town. When she showed him the fragments she clutched, his eyes widened. Despite the extreme heat of what was by then late afternoon, they jumped into a truck, drove quickly to Sharkey Williams' fence line, and then ran the next two miles across the adjoining ranch to her discovery. Crawling up to the spot Hendrickson pointed out, Larson immediately concluded that they were looking at remains of a *T. rex*. What was more, because of the manner in which the vertebrae were arranged— they seemed to form a curve that appeared to come out of and disappear back into the wall—Hendrickson's hope that more of the skeleton would be found farther back in the wall seemed well founded.

Almost giddy with excitement, Larson and Hendrickson immediately began to lay plans as to what to do next. They agreed that they must take action at once to protect her spectac- ular find. Time was of the essence, because winter is severe and often comes on suddenly in the Dakotas. Cold, icy winds and snow would make it impossible to dig. Hendrickson and Larson knew that they could not put off digging until spring; if they did so, nature might intervene—that section of the cliff wall might erode, causing fossils to fall and smash. They wanted to take fast action, to begin to search for the rest of the skeleton Larson felt sure they would find. That same night, having double-checked that Hendrickson had indeed been on land belonging to Maurice Williams, they called him to ask for formal permission to return to his land with the crew to excavate. Larson later recalled Williams as agreeing at once, as long as the crew continued to come on foot.[9]

Over the weekend, Hendrickson, as well as Pete, Matt, and Jason Larson, and Terry Wentz, returned to the cliff to look at the find. Following Peter Larson and Wentz's lead, everybody called the skeleton "Sue," following the time-honored paleontological tradition of naming a specimen after its discoverer. Cameras in hand, they photographed and videotaped the bones that were visible and recorded their exact location. Pete called his brother Neal, a partner in his business, and asked him to come as quickly as possible with equipment and supplies but refused to reveal what they were needed for.

Now the real work began. Even Hendrickson, who had spent the majority of her adult years living in less-than-comfortable conditions and was accustomed to hard physical labor, described the conditions under which they labored as cruel. They worked from dawn to dusk in an area completely without shade in temperatures that rose to 125 degrees Fahrenheit.[10]

The crew started by picking up all the fragments that had fallen, placing them one by one in plastic bags, which they painstakingly labeled. They collected dirt from the base of the cliff to screen later, in case they had missed seeing something. Moving up the cliff wall, they stabilized the bones that stuck out with glue and covered them with plaster bandages. Next they moved 30 feet up the cliff wall from the level where the bones stuck out. Working down the rock, they used picks and shovels to remove weathered, crumbling sandstone and soil, what the experts call overburden, from the front of the cliff wall. A foot back, they encountered solid rock. Slowly, Pete and Neal Larson and Hendrickson continued working down the cliff until they had formed a shelf that went 29 feet back. Just two feet above the bones, they traded their picks for rock hammers, which they used to remove the last layers of rock encasing the bones.

To their utter joy, their hard labor paid off when their digging yielded the most complete and best preserved *T. rex* skeleton ever discovered. It seems that when Sue died her corpse was almost immediately covered by sand and mud. Very few of her parts were carried away by scavengers or otherwise lost. The excavators' excitement grew when they measured Sue's bones. With a femur 54 inches long, Sue also proved to be the biggest *T. rex* ever found. She stood 13 feet tall at the hip and measured 42 feet from her brow to the tip of her tail. She would have weighed seven tons when she was alive. This makes her significantly bigger than even the awe-inspiring *T. rex* skeleton on display at the American Museum of Natural History.[11]

For 17 days, Pete Larson, Hendrickson, and Wentz labored on. As they worked, they kept a meticulous record of what they found and where they found it, making a giant map on which they traced bones at full scale. Slowly, they filled in the details as they found bone after bone. Nearly the whole body was laid out in front of them. Only one part was missing, but it was a hugely important part: the skull.

Not wanting to jinx their chances, the crew refused even to say the word "skull." When someone found a new bone, Peter Larson would only ask if it was the "s-bone."[12] On August 27, they were overjoyed when, digging down around the sides of the pelvis, Larson came across what he knew at once was the skull.[13] Their normal process of removing bones one by one, wrapping them in foil, and jacketing them in plaster would not be possible with the skull, because it lay in dangerous proximity to the pelvis.[14]

Afraid they might damage these bones if they tried to separate them out in the field, they left those bones in a gigantic four-ton block of rock that covered in plaster, reinforced with planks of wood, and finally cut loose from the surrounding rock. By September 1, everything was ready to be moved.

Maurice Williams had agreed to allow the BHI crew to bring a truck onto his land in order to remove Sue because she was far too big to be carried out. When all the work was done, Larson and the team brought in a flatbed trailer and two more trucks to carry out the bones. As a huge thunderstorm approached, he, Hendrickson, and others used a come-along to winch the enormous block of rock onto the truck. Once all the other pieces were also loaded, they drove to the Black Hills Institute in Hill City.

The next morning, Larson and Hendrickson left the rest of the BHI staff to get to work on Sue indoors. They drove to Bozeman, Montana, to show their colleague Jack Horner, a *T. rex* specialist at the Museum of the Rockies, photos of Sue's excavation. Horner had completed the excavation of another fine *T. rex* specimen earlier in the summer, so the three found it quite exciting to compare notes. Together, they discussed what would happen to Sue next. Larson had decided as soon as Sue was discovered that she would stay at Black Hills Institute. He had long planned to found a museum in Hill City, South Dakota. For 20 years, in fact, BHI had been saving all of its best specimens for this museum. Sue made this a much more exciting project. Of course, there was an enormous amount of preparation and research that would have to take place first.

Hendrickson, satisfied that Sue was in good hands, had reached the point at which she was ready to turn her attention to something else. She knew when she left that BHI would constantly give her news of how the cleaning progressed and what they were learning about Sue. She felt that she had done her part.

There was another reason Hendrickson was ready to move on: by now she was already due to move on to her next project,

While Sue Hendrickson was working in the Ruth Mason Quarry, her eyes were continually drawn to a cliff on Maurice Williams' adjoining property. When she had the opportunity to venture over and inspect the rock, she discovered the amazing *T. rex* skeleton that would later bear her name. Afraid to damage the skull of the fossil by digging it out from the surrounding rock while they were still in the quarry, the crew moved the entire of block of stone to a different location to free the skull.

a completely different sort of endeavor—marine archaeology. From the age of 20, Hendrickson had paid her bills by working as a professional diver. It was while diving for tropical fish that she had her first chance to do underwater salvage, and salvage led her to marine archaeology. She had always been paid for diving, but a lot of paleontology digs provided no more than expenses. She worked part of every year as a lobster fisherman to earn enough money to allow her to volunteer on the dinosaur digs. Her work in the Badlands complete, she was ready to head back underwater.

In the meantime, BHI started to work on Sue. In October 1991, Larson gave a talk at the Fifty-First Annual Meeting of the

Society of Vertebrate Paleontologists. He told them of the startling discoveries that had already been made with the fossil, describing her nearly complete tail (the *T. rexes* discovered before Sue had only parts of theirs), the duck-billed dinosaur bones that had been found in her stomach, and the evidence that this *T. rex* had sustained a number of horrible injuries in its life but had apparently recovered from them all. Announcing that he had no plans to sell Sue, he invited other paleontologists to inspect the skeleton.[15] Soon, he reported that he, in conjunction with Dr. Eberhard Frey of the Karlsruhe Museum in Germany, had concluded that Sue was very possibly female. Up to that point, everyone had assumed she was male. Imagine Hendrickson's excitement when she learned that "the biggest, baddest, carnivorous beast that ever walked on earth very likely was a female!"[16]

Unfortunately, Hendrickson would learn some discouraging news regarding Sue in May 1992. Soon after the excavation of Sue had started, Peter Larson had given Maurice Williams a check for $5,000. To this day, Larson and Williams disagree as to what the check was for. Larson understood it to be payment in full for the skeleton, whereas Williams later said in a letter to BHI that he "only allowed [Larson] to remove it and clean it and prepare it for sale."[17] At any rate, in 1992, a four-way fight began over who was the legal owner of Sue. BHI and Williams first staked their claims. Then, in April 1992, the Cheyenne River Sioux stated for the public record that "the world's largest *Tyrannosaurus rex*" had been stolen from their tribe, because Williams was one-eighth Sioux by birth and his ranch is on the Cheyenne River Reservation.[18]

On May 14, 1992, claiming to act on behalf of the Sioux tribe, a dozen Federal Bureau of Investigation (FBI) agents, backed by armed National Guardsmen, went to BHI before the Institute opened its doors for the day and seized the skeleton. Within two weeks, however, the federal government changed the search warrant and charged BHI with stealing the skeleton from the federal government. They based this new charge on the fact that in 1969 Williams had put his land in trust to the U.S. Department of the Interior for 25 years to excuse him from paying property taxes.[19]

The ensuing legal battle was long and bitter. Peter and Neal Larson were brought up on criminal charges. Hendrickson found herself in the awful position of having to testify in a court about Peter Larson's collecting methods. Finally, a federal judge ruled that Maurice Williams owned Sue. A jury convicted Peter Larson and sent him to prison for failing to fill out customs forms (Larson had not declared $5,000 he had carried on a collecting trip to Peru when he re-entered the United States). Williams entered into negotiations with three different museums but finally decided to sell Sue to the highest bidder, handing her over to Sotheby's, one of the world's most famous auction houses.

The auction, like the court cases, would make headlines around the world. Three hundred spectators, Hendrickson among them, watched the bidding. Bids quickly climbed from $500,000 into the millions. The hammer went down when a secret bidder, later revealed to be the Field Museum of Natural History in Chicago, offered $7.62 million.[20] Using donations from both McDonald's and the Walt Disney Company, the Field acquired Sue knowing that she would generate enough income for the museum—through the sale of admission tickets as well as souvenirs and spin-off merchandise—to fund not only a full study of her but also many of its other programs. Today, Sue is the museum's centerpiece, making the Field a place that anyone seriously interested in dinosaurs must visit.

Hendrickson had been hoping that somehow the Black Hills Institute could manage to buy Sue. When they could not come up with the funds, she was pleased that her find went to the Field.[21] Never has she felt any regret that she did not profit from her discovery; she never expected to do so. Paleontologists and collectors in the field know that whatever they find, no matter how valuable, will go to the institution for which they

Hendrickson and her beloved dog, Skywalker, are dwarfed by a cast of Sue in Washington, D.C., as part of a traveling exhibit. Although Sue was ultimately not returned to the Black Hills Institute, Hendrickson was pleased to see the fossil go to the Field Museum of Chicago, one of the world's foremost natural history museums.

work or volunteer. Throughout her long career as an explorer and adventurer, Hendrickson has always chosen to work freelance, even though doing this type of work means that she never makes a great deal of money. When a project interests her enough, she is happy to volunteer, foregoing a paycheck in favor of work she finds satisfying.

Finding Sue got Hendrickson's name in the news. Yet fame, like fortune, is something she never desired or pursued. In fact, she has always avoided the limelight. To this day, she says she would like to avoid the attention she receives as Sue's discoverer, but she has come to accept that the public wants to know more about "the lucky person who found this great *T. rex.*"[22] She has been especially accommodating to the Field when it has approached her to speak about Sue, but she can bring herself only to make rare appearances. When she does appear in public, she never delivers speeches, preferring simply to answer questions put to her. When talking with children, she encourages them to seek out adventure, and to get involved in whatever they have an "inkling of what [they] most want to do."[23]

Reflecting on her life, Hendrickson has summed up what has given her the most fulfillment, saying in her straightforward manner, "Finding is the thing." It is her interest in the search that has put Hendrickson in the ranks of the world's most successful modern explorers.

2

A Hard Time Fitting In

1949–1965

It was early in her life that Sue Hendrickson struck out on her own course, a course that has sometimes been difficult and dangerous.

Sue Hendrickson was born on December 2, 1949, in Chicago, Illinois, to Lee and Mary Hendrickson. At the time of her birth, her father had already begun what would prove to be a long and successful career as a railroad purchasing agent. He was the executive who oversaw the acquisition of raw materials

Mary and Lee Hendrickson were married in 1946 and had three children: John, Susan, and Karen. Although Mary was herself afraid of the water, she encouraged her children to learn how to swim and even campaigned to have a neighborhood swimming pool installed for her children to enjoy. Perhaps no one benefited more from Mary's efforts than her middle child, who would grow up to become one of the world's most famous divers.

for a company that manufactured train cars. Hendrickson remembers sitting at rail crossings watching trains with dozens of cars go by, calling out every time she saw one emblazoned with the code GATX (General American Transportation Company), which meant it was "my dad's."[24]

Before her marriage, Mary Hendrickson also worked as a professional. As a young woman, she taught public school, but during World War II, she went to work for American Airlines, where she rose through the administrative ranks to a high position. She resigned after she became pregnant with her first child, Sue's older brother. Until Sue was 10, Mary was a stay-at-home mom, believing that her family needed her full-time.[25]

When Sue was born, the family lived in an apartment in Chicago. Before she learned to walk, however, the Hendricksons moved to Munster, a suburb located only a few miles from the Chicago city limits but in a different state—Indiana. Once settled in Munster, the Hendrickson family expanded again, this time to include a Sue's sister Karen.

By the time she was ready for school, Sue had developed into a shy child who felt happiest by herself. Her mother made arrangements for her to go to other children's houses, but if Mary did not actually walk Sue into the house for a birthday party, for example, Sue would feel so self-conscious that she would be unable to go in. She preferred sitting alone on a neighbor's steps to going in to join a birthday party.[26] When she walked through a hall at school or down one of her town's streets, she liked to keep her head down so she wouldn't have to meet the eyes of passersby.

It seems that this is how Hendrickson developed the powers of observation that have served her so well. As a little girl, she looked for things as she walked, often finding small treasures such as coins. One of her earliest memories is of going into the alley behind her house, where every family had a wire cage in which they threw paper and other materials to burn. One day she walked along, looking through the neighbors' wire burners,

Sue, John, and Karen Hendrickson pose after a successful fishing trip while visiting their grandparents in Fort Lauderdale, Florida, in 1954. At this time in her childhood, Sue was a shy child who was developing a knack for finding things.

and spotted a small, perfect perfume bottle made of brass and decorated with a tiny white heart. Cherishing such discoveries, she developed another attribute she possesses to this day: She became a collector.

In 1955, the time had come for school. Her parents enrolled her in Munster's public elementary. A good student and obedient child, she received frequent praise from her teachers. As she grew older, she read a great deal for pleasure, easily consuming a book a day, including great works of classic literature. In their free time, she and her siblings also liked to swim. A determined woman, Mary Hendrickson had coordinated a drive to have a swimming pool built in Munster when her children were young. She herself suffered from a fear of water, which she did not want them to inherit, and Sue's father had been a high school and university swimming and diving champion.

From the beginning, Sue found the water to be an extremely comfortable environment. As she neared adolescence, her mother pushed her to join a swim team. Despite the fact that Sue excelled at swimming and won all her races, "I hated every minute of the competition." Explaining further, she has said, "[competing] against others (and having people watch me!) was something I never wanted to do."[27] On the other hand, she greatly enjoys challenging herself, pushing herself to do better.

Her mother later described this middle child as always "too bright and too far ahead to fit in."[28] By the time Sue became a teenager in the early 1960s, she was quietly rebellious.

In 1965, Hendrickson was a 16-year-old junior in high school. Sue was bored in school. She was also disappointed in her hometown, feeling that its residents were snobby and pretentious. Sue was generally tired of what she regarded as the "vanilla" life of her all-white suburb. Reflecting on her youth years later, she has written that she was lucky to have grown up where she did, but at the time, she suffered from "itchy feet"[29] and could not wait to get away from Munster. Craving independence, she worked a variety of jobs and used the money she earned to take trips out of Munster. She would go into a neighborhood called Old Town in Chicago to listen to music, out to O'Hare Airport to watch the planes come and go, or to the beach for a long walk in the winter. Sometimes she simply got in the car and drove backcountry roads for an afternoon. She always wanted to get away and be alone. At home, she tried to stimulate her mind by reading Russian novels, German philosophers, and the words of Buddha.[30]

As she approached her senior year, Sue's main goal in life was to see the world. Hoping a change of scenery would make her happier, her parents agreed that she could finish high

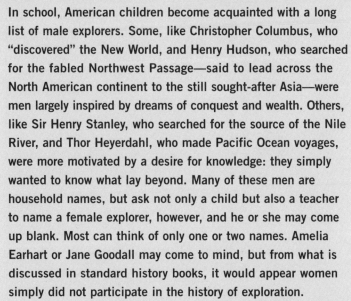

WOMEN EXPLORERS

In school, American children become acquainted with a long list of male explorers. Some, like Christopher Columbus, who "discovered" the New World, and Henry Hudson, who searched for the fabled Northwest Passage—said to lead across the North American continent to the still sought-after Asia—were men largely inspired by dreams of conquest and wealth. Others, like Sir Henry Stanley, who searched for the source of the Nile River, and Thor Heyerdahl, who made Pacific Ocean voyages, were more motivated by a desire for knowledge: they simply wanted to know what lay beyond. Many of these men are household names, but ask not only a child but also a teacher to name a female explorer, however, and he or she may come up blank. Most can think of only one or two names. Amelia Earhart or Jane Goodall may come to mind, but from what is discussed in standard history books, it would appear women simply did not participate in the history of exploration.

In recent years, however, women's studies scholars and other researchers have come across and publicized many stories of women who undertook voyages of discovery, whether they actually set off for the wilderness or into stacks at a library. Milbry Polk, for example, found 84 women explorers to write about for her book *Women of Discovery*. The women she learned about impressed her, Polk has said, not just by what they did, but what they had to overcome in order to take the first step on their journey. Typically lacking an advanced education, receiving little encouragement, and possessing only limited funds, they nevertheless set out seeking to find out for themselves a little more about the world we live in. Sue Hendrickson, although notable in her own right, turns out to be just one of many female explorers well worth finding out about.

Although a shy and introspective teenager, Sue was still fascinated by the world outside her—particularly the world outside Munster. Pictured here in a high school yearbook photo at around 16 years of age, Sue was ready to embark on a lifelong adventure that would take her out of her bland town and bring her around the world.

school in Florida, where she would live with an aunt and uncle. Even though Sue has always liked living near the ocean, she failed to settle down. She found the high school in Fort

Lauderdale even less challenging than the one she had left behind. She continued to be plagued by "the old need to roam." [31] Finally, she decided to drop out of school. She informed her aunt and uncle she was going to move to California and headed out on the road with her boyfriend. Today, she acknowledges that what she did was risky. At the time, though, she thought only of her desire for knowledge and not the dangers she might face.

3

Diving
1966–1973

At the age of 17, Sue Hendrickson left behind her safe, secure, and boring existence. With just $25 between them, she and her boyfriend went first to Lafitte, Louisiana, where they planned to look for work on a shrimp boat.[32] He loved to dive and she loved the water in general, so they thought that port town would be the perfect locale for them. When Sue had to fend off a rape by a drunken man their very first night there, however, they decided to move on.

For the next year, they lived like modern-day nomads, moving frequently from city to city.[33] They picked up odd jobs when they needed money. In the 1960s, an era in which much of America's youth rebelled against authority, many young people broke away from their parents' ways. Some were college students who participated in campus demonstrations against the Vietnam War and segregation. Others—like Sue and her boyfriend—chose to abandon the mainstream and search for new ways to live.

Life on the road was often romantic and exciting, but it proved hard, too: Hendrickson lived a largely hand-to-mouth existence, having only basic necessities. Once, in San Francisco, she found herself down to 30 cents. She had to pawn her watch—which she had inherited from her great aunt—in order to eat. She was later lucky enough to earn the money to go back and redeem it. Finally, tired of life on the road, she and her boyfriend began to think about settling down. They wanted to live in Marin County, California, but rents were extremely high there and they couldn't afford an apartment. Because they were both drawn to the water, they thought about buying a sailboat to live on, whose payments would be less expensive than most apartment rents. Hendrickson borrowed money from her parents to serve as a down payment on a 30-foot sailboat.

They berthed the boat first in Sausalito and then later at a marina in San Rafael, California. Living at the marina, they met other boat people. They started to hire out their services, painting and varnishing other people's crafts and were relieved not to have to worry about money and where they were going to sleep the next night. Hendrickson also appreciated the healthy lifestyle she enjoyed on the boat, spending hours outside every day and being surrounded by the ocean. As she later wrote, "I fell in love with everything about the ocean: the taste of the salt water, the warmth of the sun, the gentle rolling of the waves as they rocked me to sleep each night." [34]

It was also during this time that Hendrickson found a compelling new interest. In a neighborhood near the marina, there was a fish store where people went to stock their saltwater aquariums. Hendrickson was mesmerized by the vividly colored and exotic tropical fish sold there. Brimming over with curiosity, she showered the store's owner with questions. She remembers the excitement she felt when he told her that he did not breed his fish, but that someone else caught and shipped them to him. Captivated by the idea of diving for fish, Hendrickson decided to try it herself after she and her boyfriend broke up. She moved back to Florida, which is the best place in the continental United States to dive for tropical fish.

In the Florida Keys, islands off the southern coast of the state, Hendrickson was hired by two divers with a thriving tropical fish business. "I loved spending eight, nine hours in the water. It was a whole other world," she once told reporter Bruce Frankel, trying to explain why the job appealed to her. [35] What she lacked in experience she more than made up for in hard work and her ability to learn quickly. Sometimes she went under the water equipped with a hookah rig. (In hookah diving, a regulator is used to breathe underwater for an extended period of time. Compressed air comes from a small air compressor located on a boat or dock. A floating hose allows the diver to move 200 feet from the compressor.) She also used scuba gear, when needed to dive further away from the boat, or whenever there was a strong current.

Hendrickson, pictured with her dog Quincy, was able to borrow money from her parents to purchase a 30-foot sailboat, "Colleen," which she and her boyfriend lived on while they were in California. The pair adopted the lifestyle of boat living, working on other people's boats during the day and sleeping on their own at night.

Her time underwater was limited only by the amount of air she carried. The three divers spent long days underwater, stopping only at night to eat and sleep before going out to dive again the next day. Every Friday, after they packaged their catches in plastic bags that they placed in Styrofoam boxes, Hendrickson would drive their cargo to the Miami airport for shipment all over the world. Some of the fish went to wholesalers and ended up in people's homes or offices, and others went to places such as the Shedd Aquarium in Chicago and Vancouver Aquarium in Vancouver, Canada.

Although she found diving for fish deeply satisfying, Hendrickson gave it up after a year to move to Seattle, where her family had settled. Even in the big city, she managed to find a way to make money from her love of the ocean—making sails for sailboats. Spurred on by Mary Hendrickson, who had hoped that her middle child would go back to school, Sue earned her GED, or General Equivalency Diploma, officially completing her high school education. She then thought about enrolling at the University of Washington. When she went to interview there, however, she met with a professor who helped her understand that she could spend seven years earning a doctorate in marine biology, but that the only work she would

THE FLORIDA KEYS

The Florida Keys is the name given to a long string of barrier islands—there are about 1,700—that arch south and west of the Florida mainland for 220 miles. Visitors flock to not only Key Largo, the largest of the Key islands, but to many of the smaller ones as well to see picturesque beaches, mangrove forests, and other types of scenic beauty. Many come especially to participate in water sports or to fish. Lately, the Keys have attracted many ecotourists—people who want to get back to nature on vacation—as well.

Just off the Keys lies North America's only coral barrier reef. Ranked third among the world's reefs in terms of length, this reef is a very special—and very fragile—ecosystem, home not only to many species of coral, but also to tropical and other fish. Today, the federal government has declared most of the waters off the Keys part of Florida Keys National Marine Sanctuary, which protects not only the reef, but also underwater fringing mangrove stands and sea grass meadows. Diving is now restricted to certain areas prevent damage to the reef.

likely do was to dissect fish or take pollution counts. As that kind of work was not interesting to Hendrickson, she decided to return to diving and collecting tropical fish, which was immensely exciting to her and constantly provided new things to discover.

Once she became a celebrity and journalists requested interviews with her, they often ask her how she managed to become an expert in not just one but several fields of scientific study given her lack of an advanced degree. Reacting in her commonsense way, she has made it clear that this attitude—the presumption that one can only be well versed in a subject if one possesses a diploma—seems foolish to her. She once commented, "People make such a big deal of the dropout thing" and then went on to explain that her own fund of knowledge could be easily explained: "I've got a good, logical mind, and I teach myself."[37] Anyone who learns about Hendrickson's life might add that there seems to be more to the story: Hendrickson also possesses a seemingly endless curiosity and great self-discipline, a combination that makes it easy for her to learn on her own. Whenever she encounters a topic that interests her, she generally does two things. First, she reads up, doing background research in books and journals. Second, she seeks out the experts who can answer questions that arise. Over time, she found that not only does this help satisfy her own curiosity, but it also sometimes helps her land a job.

4

Marine
Archaeology
1973–1983

After living in Seattle for a year, Sue Hendrickson moved back to Florida where she returned to diving for a living, this time with a new diving partner, a retired Navy Seal. As always, she felt at home in the water, and continued to be fascinated by diving because it seemed as if every time she dived underwater she saw something new. Over time, she and her business partner came across some very "weird" fish. She took their truly unusual finds to experts at the NOAA—the National Oceanic and Atmospheric Administration, which has offices on Virginia Key in Miami—or to the Rosenstiel School of Marine and Atmospheric Science at the University of Miami. Fish, shark, and invertebrate specialists truly enjoyed examining her finds, some of which proved to be species that had never been identified. Hendrickson contributed to science, and in turn, the scientists taught her a great deal about everything from nomenclature to anatomy.

By 1973, Hendrickson had a wide circle of friends in Florida who shared her interest in the ocean. Some of them were divers like her, others were fishers and sailors. One day, when visiting a friend who worked for a salvage company, a freighter ran aground on a reef in the Florida Keys. Because the company was short-handed, Hendrickson was asked to join the crew. The ship contained valuable cargo of building materials that the owner wanted saved, and the freighter needed to be removed to minimize damage to the reef. Coral feels hard and looks sturdy, but it is actually extremely fragile. Even a slight touch can damage or kill sensitive coral polyps.[38]

Hendrickson leaped at the chance when she was asked to join this job. This freighter was Hendrickson's first salvage job; later, she also helped bring up boats, airplanes, and cars that had somehow come to be underwater, sometimes at great depths. Because each job is different, and typically difficult, salvage work requires mental ingenuity. Hendrickson has described Chet Alexander—head of Alexander Marine Salvage of Key West, for which she worked—as a great puzzle solver.

(continued on page 34)

SALVAGE MISSIONS

It was while doing salvage work that Hendrickson learned many of the skills she needed in the next field she explored: marine archaeology. Humans have been trying to retrieve cargo lost in shipwrecks for ages. The early effort we know most about was by Leon Battista Alberti. In the mid-fifteenth century, he received a commission from Cardinal Colonna, who collected Greek and Roman art, to search for two Roman ships said to have sunk in Lake Nemi, located east of Rome. This lake was important because the Temple of Diana was built on its shores. Historians speculate that the emperor Caligula ordered the ships built for use in the religious ceremonies in which he worshipped the Egyptian god Isis in the first century A.D. Alberti's search for the sunken ships began in 1446 and involved a dozen swimmers who had to locate the ships at a depth of ten fathoms (approximately 18 meters). Alberti attempted to raise the ships but failed. Divers were able to bring up only a few planks of wood and a statue.

In 1535, Francesco Pemarchi invented a very primitive diving suit. (This is the first known to have been made.) It worked well enough for him to get a good look at the ships and to take their measurements, but he could do no more. It was not until 1827 that eight people went to the bottom of Lake Nemi in a diving bell. They managed to bring up more fragments of wood, marble, and some mosaics. Still later, in 1895, Eliseo Borghi, an antiquities dealer, brought up larger pieces of the ships, but in the process he damaged one of their hulls.* Only when the lake was drained in the early 1920s, under the orders of the Italian dictator Benito Mussolini, were the rest of the barges finally exposed and salvaged. Study of them ended in 1944 because German troops burned them during World War II.**

In the meantime, there were other attempts at marine salvage of historic artifacts. In 1853, members of the Zurich

Antiquarian Society used "grabs" attached to the bottom of poles to bring up Bronze Age artifacts, including axes, chisels, flint knives, bracelets, reed mats, fabric, and nets, from the bottoms of several different lakes.

Significant advances in diving equipment were made in the nineteenth century. The British navy became intensely involved in the development of diving gear because it wanted to retrieve cannons from the HMS *Royal George*, which had sunk in 1783 while carrying 108 guns. In 1834, a navy diver wore a suit with an unattached helmet invented by Charles and John Deane and descended the 65 feet to explore the *Royal George* wreck. The unattached helmet meant that he had to stand upright at all times, never bending over. This made extensive work underwater impossible. Three years later, Augustus Siebe found a way to attach a helmet to a diving suit.***

Joseph Cabirol created great excitement among those interested in diving when he showed a diving suit to which a secure helmet with four portholes could be attached at the Exposition Universelle in Paris. A hose attached close to the right ear brought in air from a tank on the surface. A valve allowed the diver to adjust how much air he received. A second hose was attached at the mouth; it was there for safety reasons, because it allowed the diver to whistle for help if in trouble. A showman by nature, Cabirol went to great lengths to publicize his invention: He made headlines when he lowered a convicted felon to a depth of 40 meters (131 feet) in his suit. Still, no one was able to overcome the problems associated with going deeper. Divers suffered from the bends or decompression sickness, and those who rose to the surface too quickly suffered embolisms.[†]

Only in the twentieth century did diving become popular. The general public began to display interest in underwater exploration and marine archaeology around the middle of the century because of efforts of one of the most inventive scientists of our time, Jacques Cousteau, who sought to educate the public about life in the ocean. Cousteau used an airlift to suck up mud from sunken shipwrecks. This helped clean off wrecks so divers could get to artifacts without having to move what was sometimes tons of sand and mud. The mud brought up to the surface was forced through strainers to make sure no artifacts were lost.

Cousteau did some underwater surveying of archaeological sites, but he was not systematic. He is credited with being the first to use underwater communications telephones to issue instructions to divers and closed-circuit televisions to observe excavation as it proceeded. Because special under-water cameras took a long time to appear, he faced a serious problem in getting photos of sites.

In the 1950s, for the first time, a systematic survey of a wreck was made when the *Spargi*, a Roman ship that went down in the first century B.C., was excavated in the Mediterranean.[††] Nino Lamboglia developed what would become a standard marine archaeology technique when he used pegs and yellow tape to create grids over a wreck and then photographed the grid square by square to create a guide to where the objects found lay in relation to one another.

In 1964, the University of Pennsylvania, the National Geographic Society, and the National Science Foundation joined forces to develop *Alvin*, a tiny electric two-person submarine that was equipped with two synchronized cameras. Unfortunately, *Alvin* proved so expensive to maintain that it had to be sold to a company that serviced offshore oil rigs (although scientists can still lease the sub). Today, hundreds of sunken vessels have been excavated. They have yielded information about life on ships, cargoes, trade routes, and early metallurgy and glass making.

Sue Hendrickson joined the field at a time when it was burgeoning, as Jacques Cousteau reached the height of his popularity. In 1974, Hendrickson signed on to take part in a marine archaeology expedition to Colombia. A financier had put up money to sponsor some treasure diving. En route, the group, which included seven divers including Hendrickson, stopped in the Dominican Republic, which, along with Haiti, is located on an island in Caribbean Sea. This island was the place where Christopher Columbus first made landfall in the New World in 1492. Claiming it for his sponsors, the king and queen of Spain, he named it Hispaniola, a name that is rarely used now. In the sixteenth century, Hispaniola served as a "springboard" from which Spanish conquistadors and soldiers set out to explore and conquer other New World lands. [†††] France established a claim to the western third of the island—Haiti—in 1697. Spain remained in control of the remainder until 1821, when the Haitians picked up arms to fight for their own independence. After they also succeeded in getting Spain to relinquish its claims to Hispaniola, Haitians ruled the entire island until 1844, when it once again became two separate nations, with the Dominican Republic in the east and Haiti in the west.

[*] Underwater Archaeology Glossary, *http://www.abc.se/~m10354/uwa/ glossary.htm#don't%20touch.*

[**] Lake Nemi Ships, Underwater Archaeology Glossary, http://www.abc.se/~m10354/mar/nemships.htm.

[***] Mark V. Lonsdale, Evolution of US Navy Diving, *http://www.navydiver.org/history/default.html.*

[†] The First Diving Suits, *http://www.culture.fr/culture/archeosm/archeosom/en/scafan.htm.*

[††] John Illsley, "Spargi," History and Archaeology of the Ship, *http://cma.soton.ac.uk/HistShip/shlect43.htm.*

[†††] Dominican Republic Factbook, CIA World Factbook Page, *http://www.cia.gov/cia/publications/factbook/geos/dr.html.*

Hendrickson holds a compass she brought up from a shipwreck while doing salvage work in Florida in 1974. Hendrickson became quite skilled at salvaging, and eventually worked on jobs from centuries-old shipwrecks to recent airplane crashes.

(continued from page 29)

In addition to clear and creative thinking, salvage work also demands tremendous physical effort. After one job in which a ship had to be towed off a reef, both of Hendrickson's big toenails fell off because she had banged and bruised her feet so badly. Another of her great salvage stories occurred when she was staying on Alexander's towing barge. She was awakened by a midnight phone call asking the company to handle an emergency. While a tugboat was towing an oil barge, the barge's tow line became caught in the tugboat's propellors, and the two crafts were drifting toward the reef. Hendrickson and Alexander went out to the immobile boats on his salvage barge, intending to tow the tugboat and the oil barge back to port. Hendrickson and Alexander's own towline became entangled in their propeller, and because they had expected this to be a straight-forward job, they had not stopped to pick up any diving gear. Afraid of sharks, none of the crew members of the drifting boats wanted to get in the water, so Hendrickson was the one to dive under the barge and free the towline. It took her an hour to cut through just one of the towline's three strands. By the end of the night, she was exhausted, but the job was done.

It made Hendrickson proud not only to salvage people's property, but also to help the environment. Chet Alexander has since died, but his long-time first mate C.A. Paxton has taken the business, which remains highly successful. Hendrickson herself has remarked that Alexander Marine has an amazing safety record. In 40 years, Alexander and his crew found them-selves in some life-or-death situations, but there had never been a death resulting from one of his salvage operations.

Hendrickson turned her attention from the Florida Keys to the Dominican Republic, the site of many shipwrecks. The group Hendrickson planned on joining on a dive of a Spanish shipwreck made every attempt to persuade the government to permit them to do so, visiting offices and beseeching officials. Unfortunately, the group never got the permit required. Nevertheless, Hendrickson did not consider her trip there a waste of time because she fell in love with the island and made some friends she still has today. In fact, after she returned to Florida, she went back to the Dominican Republic whenever she could save up enough money (it did not require a lot—she found she could live there extremely cheaply, two dollars a day covering both a room and food).

Hendrickson became interested in amber, particularly those pieces containing insects, while living in the Dominican Republic. Finding the work of mining amber far less rewarding than the act of collecting it, Hendrickson instead meets with natives and purchases pieces from them.

While continuing to both do salvage and sign on for more marine archaeology work, in the mid-1970s Hendrickson found a brand-new interest. One day while on a trip into the Dominican mountains with some friends, she visited an amber mine, where natives were collecting the fossilized resin of ancient trees. Most collectors like the orange amber that is clear (this clear amber is often made into jewelry), but what grabbed

Hendrickson's attention were the pieces that included an insect that had become caught in the resin and then preserved as it hardened over millions of years. Fascinated, she started to work on a collection of her own, going from mine to mine to purchase specimens. For a time, she tried mining herself, but she found it too time-consuming. Speaking from experience, she has said, "You could dig for months and find nothing in the Dominican caves. [So instead of digging] I buy it from the locals who mine it." Making a list of her favorite pieces, she thinks of her butterflies (of the six in total that have been found thus far, she at one point owned three—she has since sold or donated them all to museums), tarantulas, a single piece with two scorpions, and some examples in which tiny vertebrates are trapped. Typically, she added one or two new species to her collection every trip. Making four or five trips a year, she could end a year with several spectacular new finds, which she sent off to experts to be studied.

5

Fossils
1983–1985

Over and over again in Sue Hendrickson's life, one passion has led to another. As a result of her love of amber, she became interested in the field of fossils. Fossils, the remains of ancient plants and animals, are of great interest to both amateur naturalists and professional scientists because of the information they yield about the earth in earlier eras.

The first fossils were discovered by accident. Today, a significant number—perhaps even the majority—are still found by chance. Many end up in the hands of private individuals who do not engage in any serious study of them. Others, however, have been deliberately sought out. Since the eighteenth century, those individuals interested in science have sponsored expeditions and exchanged information about the finds.

Hendrickson's interest in fossils evolved from the particular to the general. For a time, amber remained her sole focus. Always a "bookaholic," she delved into reference books to find out more about what she was acquiring.[39] Once she learned what was unusual, she described to native hunters what types of specimens she was especially interested in. She began building what have now become long-term relationships with amber miners in both the Dominican Republic and Mexico. Her efforts paid off. Over time, she built an outstanding collection that included both specimens of scientific significance and display-quality pieces. As she came across new types, she sent her specimens to other experts in the field. This helped her learn more, because the experts communicated their findings back to her. Gradually, she became an expert in the very specialized field of ancient entomology. Her willingness to share her findings had another result, as well: It helped her establish an enviable reputation in the museum world—curators describe her as an extremely generous individual, who, unlike some collectors, delights in sharing her finds with the wider world. She shares more than information. Over time she has helped four museums build substantial collections of amber.

Kirby Siber, Dr. Hernando de Macedo (then director of the Museo Nacional de Historia Natural de Peru), Carlos Martin, and Peter Larson were part of the team Sue Hendrickson worked with while digging for whale fossils in Peru. Hendrickson enjoyed the work so much that she returned to the Peruvian Deserts five more seasons and later joined Larson and his Black Hills Institute team on fossil hunts in South Dakota.

It was while searching for others who shared her interest in amber at a fossil and mineral show that Hendrickson set off on a new career path. There she met Kirby Siber, a Swiss mineralogist and paleontologist who, among other things, digs for fossils. He keeps most of his finds for his own large museum—the Sauriermuseum, in Aathal (near Zurich), Switzerland, which contains one of Europe's finest collections of dinosaur fossils. He sells his other discoveries to museums all over the world. Impressed by Hendrickson's natural intelligence, curiosity, knowledge, and ability to work hard, Siber soon extended her an irresistible invitation. He was living in Peru and was about to undertake a major hunt for fossils in an ancient seabed with Peter Larson of South Dakota's Black Hills Institute. When Siber asked Hendrickson to join them, she seized the chance. As she later remarked, it was the perfect project, because it "[combined] my love of the ocean and fossils."[40]

(continued on page 44)

PETER LARSON AND THE BLACK HILLS INSTITUTE

Larson, a native of South Dakota, had been interested in paleontology since childhood. His interest came in part from his surroundings: He was born and raised in a part of the world where dinosaur bones abound and some of the most significant finds of all time have been made. Looking back, Larson says he cannot remember a time when he and his brother Neal were not on the lookout for fossils. As children, they loved to arrange and display their best finds for friends and family. At an age when other kids were playing house, they played museum.

Larson knew he wanted to be a paleontologist from the time he found his first fossil at the age of four.[*] Thus it was only natural when, after graduating from high school, he enrolled at the South Dakota School of Mines, which has a reputation as one of the best schools to study geology or the closely related field paleontology. Putting himself through school by working three jobs, he had almost completed a master's thesis when he had to take some time off to work full-time and earn enough money to continue school. Thus, in 1974, he and his friend Jim

Honert established Black Hills Minerals, a company that sold the rocks and minerals Larson and Honert found to museums and universities. One year later Larson tried to reenroll in school, but the head of the geology department told him that none of his earlier credits counted and that he would have to do all the coursework again if he wanted to receive his degree.

Unable to give in to these demands, Larson instead devoted his full attention to the business, which eventually changed its name to the Black Hills Institute and added fossils to its sale lists. Soon, his focus shifted to searching specifically for dinosaurs. This happened after 1977, when Larson sold a fossil turtle to a museum in Europe. The museum indicated that it hoped to buy a dinosaur skeleton from them soon. Larson later described what transpired: "We said, 'No problem.' We didn't have a dinosaur. We didn't even know where to dig dinosaurs."***

A little while later, they were extremely fortunate to be contacted by Ruth Mason, a South Dakota woman then in her 80s who owned a large piece of property in the Hell Creek Formation. She had been convinced ever since she was a child that some of the bones she found on her property were ancient. For more than 50 years, she had been trying without success to interest paleontologists in digging on her land. The Larsons, however, leaped when she offered them that chance and were amply rewarded by their decision: They did indeed find the dinosaur bones she had promised them—in fact, in what is now known as the Ruth Mason Quarry, they found thousands upon thousands of duckbill fossils (to this day, there is no explanation as to why so many died in one place). Kirby Siber put up the money the Larsons needed to finance their dig. Excavation yielded a plenitude of duckbill bones, but it took a long time for Larson and his coworkers to piece together a complete duckbill skeleton. It was only in 1981 that they succeeded. Fulfilling the promise he had made years earlier, Larson offered the skeleton to the museum in Vienna, but it could not raise the funds he needed to pay off the $60,000 he had borrowed to finance his dig. The specimen instead went to the Ulster Museum in Belfast, which paid $150,000.

In the meantime, the Black Hills Institute was growing. Over the years, it would hold annual summer digs in which other professionals, academics (including students), and volunteers participated. Larson taught hundreds of people about paleontology. Some he introduced to fieldwork. Others learned preparation techniques and got crash courses in dinosaur science.

Over the next ten years, Larson's team would put together more museum-quality specimens. Some of their price tags reached $300,000 on dinosaurs they sold to museums in Europe, Japan, and the United States. (This is an enormous amount of money, but it would be a mistake to conclude that selling fossils was making Larson a rich man. To unearth a specimen can take thousands of man-hours and expensive equipment. Larson calculated that on that first sale, the Institute actually finally made less than one dollar per hour.) More success followed. Over time, BHI would sell or donate fossils to hundreds of museums located all over the world. Today, it is the largest fossil supplier in the world.*** Prestigious institutions, including the Smithsonian Institution, the American Museum of Natural History, and the Peabody Museum—one of the nation's oldest natural history museums, part of Yale University—seek out BHI wares for study and display. When the Royal Tyrrell Museum of Paleontology, in Alberta, Canada, opened, 95 percent of its real fossil specimens were from BHI.

* Fiffer, *Tyrannosaurus Sue*, p. 2.
** Ibid., p. 11.
*** Memo from Hendrickson to author, September 27, 2003.

Larson, Hendrickson, and Carlos Martin, another team member, unearth a baleen whale fossil in Peru. The fossils the team discovered were sent to museums all over the world. The team also built a museum at the site in Sacaco, Peru, under Kirby Siber's leadership.

(continued from page 41)

Hendrickson found working on this project so satisfying that she returned to Peru every winter (during the Southern Hemisphere's warm months) for five years. She worked for Siber for the first two seasons. After that, she and Larson collected for the Black Hills Institute, although they also helped Siber when he needed them. Hendrickson spent her summers in the Northern Hemisphere, where she continued to dive for shells to sell, as well as doing some very lucrative lobster fishing. This work gave her the money to indulge in what fast became a consuming passion: paleontology.

In Peru, she was in on spectacular finds, unearthing fossilized dolphins, seals, sharks, and whales from the Miocene epoch—10 to 20 million years ago, in the age when elsewhere on earth grasses were developing and grazing mammals appeared.

Continually finding things that had never before been seen or studied was very exciting.

In 1990, Hendrickson was engaged in what had developed into happy routine when her life took a scary turn. Concerned about unexplained vaginal bleeding, she visited her gynecologist who diagnosed her as having cervical cancer.[41] Fortunately, the cancer had yet to spread and a hysterectomy provided a cure. Hendrickson became a survivor of cancer. Unfortunately, the hysterectomy made it impossible for her to bear children, which she found sad and deeply disappointing. When Hendrickson went into surgery, she, Siber, and Larson had to postpone the opening of a museum they founded together approximately 60 miles (120 kilometers) south of Nasca, Peru. They built it around one of the huge fossilized baleen whales they had found. Enclosing the fossil in this manner guaranteed both that the specimen would be preserved and that others would see it. The opening was held as soon as Hendrickson had recovered from her surgery.

The opening of the Nasca museum marked the end of the trio's digs in Peru. By this time, however, paleontology had become as important a focus in Hendrickson's life as marine archaeology had. When Larson asked her to join the Black Hills Institute's annual summer digs in South Dakota, she knew she did not want to pass up the opportunity to look for dinosaurs in the Hell Creek Formation.

When Hendrickson joined the Black Hills Institute on its summer digs, it was a quickly expanding business. She had greatly enjoyed the digs in Peru, and she found the Badlands digs so satisfying that she sold her boat and gave up lobster fishing (dinosaur digs and lobster fishing must be undertaken during the same time—during the warm months—which made it impossible for her to do both). Soon, she had a new business: selling conch pearls, which, with her diving jobs, enabled Hendrickson to pay her bills.

6

Sue

When Hendrickson found the dinosaur fossil that would be named after her in 1990, she had no idea that she would soon be at the center of a great paleontological controversy (as debate arose concerning BHI's right to collect fossils for sale). Years earlier, Peter Larson had been appointed to the National Academy of Science's committee (whose purpose was to help the federal government formulate regulations concerning public access to fossils on government land). Other commercial collectors and amateurs regarded him as a spokesperson. Hendrickson remembers thinking, "Whew!" after the intense meetings she attended.[42] Sometimes debate became so heated between the Academy and the government that it became necessary to use a professional mediator to act as a go-between.

By 1990, Hendrickson was a full-fledged field paleontologist. She lacked a formal education in paleontology, having never done any undergraduate or graduate work, but by going out in the field, she had gained the skills she needed to be able to find and excavate specimens. (These are skills that some academic paleontologists never acquire. Those who work with bones in a museum, for example, do much more research but may never have found a bone on their own.) Asked how she acquired these skills, she provides a two-part answer, saying first that she learned a great deal by herself, just by going on her own to look, to get used to process of searching for signs of skeletons. In addition, she learned by working side by side with others who had more experience.

Hendrickson had begun by collecting fossils in Morocco intermittently from 1982 to 1985. In southern Morocco, she would search for ammonites and trilobites, and in the northern part of the country, she had searched for shark teeth. She prospected in other countries, too, looking for meteorites, fossil fish, or ancient mammals. Hendrickson remembers going out by herself or with just one or two other people.

Hendrickson wears a traditional Berber headdress during her time in Africa in the early 1980s. While in Morocco, she searched for a variety of natural treasures, from mineral specimens to the fossils of ancient sea animals and shark teeth.

When others did go along, they always split up in the morning and joined up again at night.

Beginning in 1988, she went to work at the Larsons' main dig. Since 1979, the Institute had gone back each year to the Ruth Mason Quarry. Their most important find up to this time—worthy of any paleontologist—was of a huge mass of skeletons of the *Edmontosaurus annectens,* widely known as duckbills. Working there, BHI staff learned to collect bones in exactly the right way—quickly and carefully. By developing a useful mapping technique, they were able to collect information not only about the duckbills but also about the other animals that had died on the site in the same era.

(continued on page 52)

PALEONTOLOGY

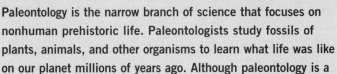

Paleontology is the narrow branch of science that focuses on nonhuman prehistoric life. Paleontologists study fossils of plants, animals, and other organisms to learn what life was like on our planet millions of years ago. Although paleontology is a relatively new field of study, dating back less than 200 years, scientists have been interested in fossils for many centuries.*

Mary Ann Mantell stumbled on a huge tooth when she was fossil hunting on England's coast in 1822. Her husband, Gideon Mantell, was an obstetrician as well as an amateur naturalist and geologist. He puzzled over the tooth and decided that it must have come from a huge reptile, the likes of which had never been imagined.

Members of the Geological Society of London scoffed, saying that what Mary Ann Mantell had discovered was from a rhinoceros. Gideon Mantell did not give up on his theory, however, and returned to where the tooth was found. The layers of the rock in which the fossil had been discovered demonstrated that the tooth was from the Mesozoic strata. On a visit to a museum, Mantell found a modern-day iguana's tooth on display and became convinced that the huge tooth in question came from a creature extremely similar in structure but 20 times greater in size. He then drew a sketch of this giant iguana and named the new species he believed they had discovered "Iguanodon."

The Mantell's discovery opened an exciting era in the history of science. By 1842, the scientific community was convinced that there had been an order of reptiles in the ancient world. British paleontologist Richard Owen proposed that the order be named "dinosauria," which translates from Latin as "terrible lizards." The hunt began.

Employed by what would become the United States Geological Survey, Ferdinand Hayden found the first dinosaur remains in North America. When he sent off his finds to scientists for study, a "dinosaur war" resulted. Two scientists in particular, Edward D. Cope and Othniel Marsh, became fierce rivals, each wanting to be regarded as the world's foremost dinosaur expert.

Marsh stayed on the East Coast at first, while Cope went west. In 1872, a mutual friend named Joseph Leidy took both men on an expedition to Wyoming. They managed to work together for a time, but the situation deteriorated again. From this point on, they both worked nonstop, competing to name and describe the most new fossil species.

Eighty years after the first dinosaur discoveries, the first tyrannosaur was found by fossil collector Barnum Brown. Brown had become so intrigued by a triceratops horn impression he had seen that he explored the part of Montana where it had been found. Brown spent the summer of 1902 digging in the Hell Creek Formation, where Hendrickson would later discover Sue. There he found incomplete remains of the previously unknown *T. rex*. Brown discovered a second specimen six years later, which included an entire skull and was thus extremely important.

Huge finds continued to be made. For a long time, most paleontological expeditions were funded by museums, often attached to universities. Estimates are, however, that more than 90 percent of all fossils in museums were found by nonacademics like Sue Hendrickson. Some were people who stumbled across fossils. Others had another line of work but possessed an avid interest in paleontology and used their free time to go out into the field and deliberately hunt for dinosaur bones. In the past, oil companies employed many paleontologists to search for fossil fuels.

Recently, commercial hunters like the Larsons have joined the search. Some hunt and sell fossils in order to afford their own collections. They do far more, however, than just pick up bones and label them with price tags. The Black Hills Institute, for example, has a laboratory and workshop where staff members prepare bones and study them. They collect documentation for the specimens. Today, few museums have a budget to send their own staff members on hunts regularly, and they often buy from the commercial enterprises.

In the past 50 years, huge strides have been made in the field of paleontology. As more and more species have been identified and studied, scientists have a greater understanding of pre-historic life. Paleontologists continue to argue amongst themselves, and they seem to actually glory in their arguments, recognizing that disagreements can lead to progress. Scientists who propose new theories must defend them, and in testing theories, fresh evidence is sometimes put forward. This can lead to the development of a whole new idea.

One current debate revolves around bones that some identify as coming from a juvenile tyrannosaur. Others believe that the bones come from a different species called the nanotyrannus, or "tiny tyrant." Other debates revolve around how dinosaurs lived. Recent finds of dinosaur nests, eggs, and infants are yielding new information about dinosaur families and how adults reared their young. Of course, the debate concerning how the dinosaurs died still rages, with some paleontologists arguing that an asteroid that hit Earth, wiping out the dinosaurs, while others contend that due to climatic and other changes, the dinosaurs gradually died out.

* Bijal P. Trivedi, "Tiny Tyrant—Fossil May be Mini *T. Rex* Cousin," *http://news.nationalgeographic.com/news/2002/08/0809_0208080_TVhadrosaur.htm*.

(continued from page 49)

They collected fossilized leaves, amber, wood, invertebrates (insects), and small vertebrates (animals with backbones) as evidence of the environment millions of years ago. Because they spent more time in the field than other paleontologists, they had especially outstanding skills. Larson had plenty of experience producing very accurate scientific specimens for a very discerning clientele—the world's leading museums—and he had contributed essays on the best collecting techniques to several books.

Hendrickson was a BHI volunteer for four summers. She has described work in the quarry as fun but very different in character than prospecting. At the quarry, everybody worked in a tightly defined space, digging around bone after bone until the bones were released one by one. Over the years, many volunteers helped out. At times, with BHI staff, amateurs, professors, and students, there might be as many as 40 people working at the quarry. At other times there were only 10 or 12.

More than once, Professor Klaus Westphal of the University of Wisconsin at Madison brought a group of students. Other groups came from the Memphis Pink Palace Museum, the University of Kansas, the New Mexico Bureau of Mines, the Denver Museum, and the Yale Peabody Museum. Kirby Siber and his crew came from Switzerland, and there were also people from numerous rock and fossil clubs. Professors liked to bring their students because work at the quarry was a very useful teaching tool. It allowed the professors to build on what their students had learned about geology and paleontology in the classroom. Television journalist Walter Cronkite even filmed a segment at the quarry for a series of specials he called "Dinosaur, The Biggest Story Ever Told."[43] At the quarry, everybody lived in tents and shared the cooking, and there was a lot of camaraderie. Hendrickson found the people at the quarry interesting but nevertheless preferred time alone in many ways.

Setting off on her own, as she had done so often in her childhood, Hendrickson explored the cliffs of the South Dakota Badlands while working with the Black Hills Institute in the Ruth Mason Quarry. It was while taking a solo hike in the Badlands that Hendrickson discovered her most famous find, Sue.

In July 1990, BHI staff and volunteers went back to the Ruth Mason Quarry for the annual digging season. Hendrickson joined them at the start. For four to six weeks (the season varied in length from one season to the next), she and the others spent their days outdoors searching for and excavating duckbill bones, laboring under harsh conditions. South Dakota, although cold in the winter, has very hot summers. The Ruth Mason Quarry is located in Badlands, a barren stretch of land characterized by eroded ridges and peaks. In 1979, Mason showed the Larsons a stretch of bluff along the Moreau River. Digging up to 18 inches deep, they found the disarticulated (unattached) bones of thousands of duckbills, or *Edmontosaurus annectens*.[44] An herbivore, or plant-eater, the "Edmonton lizard" was one of the biggest duck-billed dinosaurs; it is characterized by powerful jaws, a bulky body, small forelimbs, strong hindlimbs, and a deep tail. It resembled the Iguanodon but was larger and had a flatter nose, hundreds of close-packed cheek teeth, and inflatable skin flaps over large nasal cavities.[45]

In photographs from the Mason digs, the volunteers are dressed in jeans and ragged T-shirts, working on their hands and knees.[46] Slowly and painstakingly, they searched for fossilized bones.

By the middle of August, they were wrapping up the season. Most of the volunteers and BHI staff members headed for home. Larson, however, had one more thing he wanted to take care of before the weather changed. Larson's son, Matt, had found a triceratops skull on Sharkey Williams' ranch, which was next to the Ruth Mason Quarry.

Triceratops was a rhinoceros-like dinosaur. It walked on four sturdy legs and had three horns on its face as well as a large bony plate projecting from the back of its skull (a frill). One short horn above its beak and two longer horns (more than 3 feet long) above its eyes probably provided protection from predators. The horns were also possibly used in mating rivalry and rituals. It had a large skull, up to 10 feet long, one of the largest skulls of any land animal ever discovered. Its head was nearly one-third as long as its body. It was about 30 feet long, 10 feet tall, and weighed between 6 and 12 tons. Triceratops had a short, pointed tail, a bulky body, column-like legs with hoof-like claws, and a bony neck frill rimmed with bony bumps. It had a parrot-like beak, many cheek teeth, and powerful jaws.

Larson, Terry Wentz, Sue Hendrickson, and Larson's son and nephew set to work to investigate Matt's find. It was while working on the project that Sue Hendrickson found the *T. rex* skeleton that would come to bear her name. On August 12, 1990, when Larson, his son, his nephew, and

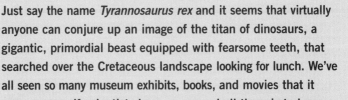

THE *T. REX*

Just say the name *Tyrannosaurus rex* and it seems that virtually anyone can conjure up an image of the titan of dinosaurs, a gigantic, primordial beast equipped with fearsome teeth, that searched over the Cretaceous landscape looking for lunch. We've all seen so many museum exhibits, books, and movies that it may seem as if scientists have uncovered all there is to know about dinosaurs. This impression is incorrect. In truth, what seems like the large amount of information we possess about the *T. rex* is based on a very small number of skeletons, bones, and fragments. When Hendrickson answered Sue's call, the number of other *T. rex* skeletons that had been located totaled only ten over 82 years. In the roughly 15 years that have passed since Sue's discovery, on the other hand, close to 20 have been found.

Today, paleontologists know a great deal about the *T. rex*. They all agree that this was the largest animal alive in its era and that it was one of the most successful predators ever to live. There are some very basic matters that the experts cannot agree on, however. For example, Jack Horner enjoys exciting arguments by claiming that the beast was actually not a hunter but a scavenger, which was like a vulture, eating the corpses of animals it found dead. Almost everyone disagrees with Horner, yet his theory gets a fair amount of attention, in part because of its outrageous quality.

Other questions concern how one might tell the difference between male and female *T. rex*es, what purpose those tiny forelegs served, and how fast they could move. All agree that *T. rex* did move faster than hadrosaurs and ceratopsians, but few believe it moved as fast as the movie *Jurassic Park* would lead one to believe.

Wentz returned from town after fixing their flat tire, Sue met them back at the site of the triceratops excavation from her hike, breathless and clutching bone fragments Larson at once recognized as having once belonged to a tyrannosaur. It was the find of a lifetime and Hendrickson, in keeping with the field paleontologist's code, made it on Larson's behalf, basically giving him Sue as a present.

Sue Hendrickson's discovery of the *T. rex* set BHI on a whole new course. In early September, the *Rapid City Journal* carried Peter and Neal Larson's first announcement of the find. They described Sue as the largest *T. rex* ever found. Sue was especially exciting to the paleontological community because she was superbly preserved, which made her extremely valuable to researchers. Her bones were nearly pristine, with only minimal crushing, and their mineralization was excellent. Much less glue was needed than usual in order to stabilize the bones.

Peter Larson described the attributes that made this find especially exciting: the size, the nearly complete torso and tail, one complete arm, and a skull that still had the lower jaw and a full set of teeth. (Very often, when an animal dies, as the body decomposes, its skull falls off. The skulls and bodies are often separated, making research difficult.) They had already found evidence of a head injury and a broken leg, and Larson speculated as to how the huge creature had healed, wondering out loud whether another *T. rex* had cared for him or her. According to the article, Sue would be the star of a new museum that the city had the highest hopes for, knowing that dinosaurs attract tourists. The museum would create more jobs and boost the local economy. Other newspapers and magazines soon picked up on the story.

In January 1991, *Discovery* magazine ran an article about another *T. rex,* this one discovered a one year earlier by Jack Horner. The article speculated about the possible use tyrannosaurs could have had for very short arms. Larson concluded

Sue Hendrickson
in Her Own Words

A Conversation with Sue Hendrickson by Milbry Polk

POLK: What has life as an explorer taught you?

HENDRICKSON: Tolerance, adaptability, courage, self-reliance and confidence. And the importance of freedom; having the freedom to make good choices when the opportunities have presented themselves. Throughout my life, I have always been on the lookout for something new and interesting to learn about. I have always had a goal, even though I sometimes switch directions in the middle of a project. That is what I mean by adaptability: the ability to recognize an opportunity and seize it. Many people don't realize an opportunity is there, or if they do, they hesitate and miss it. I have learned to lose the fear of taking that first step. That fear is what stops most people from moving forward

and learning new things. For me that fear never goes away—it just gets easier. But once you have made the move towards the unknown, the momentum builds and it is fantastic. And it cannot be refused: once you start down the path, the thrill, the interest, or the excitement is so worth it that you never go back!

POLK: What was the most difficult thing you have done?

HENDRICKSON: The most difficult things I've done have been on dives. Some were quite dangerous, but always well-thought out and under control. They were dangerous in that there was zero tolerance for error but you grow used to these "calculated risks" and make your own decisions whether to accept them or not. It all depends on your self confidence and the calmness with the upcoming efforts. Only panic can truly kill you.

POLK: Have you ever felt you had to prove yourself on expeditions?

HENDRICKSON: Well I have had to prove that I have the skills and abilities. For example, when I began working with a French archaeological diving group, I was starting from scratch, even

B

though I had years of diving experience. I had to prove myself all over again to them. I had to do everything better and longer and harder. But that project was so incredible that I could not wait to begin each day.

It probably took a couple of seasons for them to accept without question that I could accomplish as much, or more, as the team. Each of us has different talents we combine so they can be optimized in each project.

POLK: Tell us about your most famous discovery, Tyrannosaurus Sue. This dinosaur is now at the Field Museum and drawing record crowds.

HENDRICKSON: Finding Sue was awesome. I still don't believe that I found such a great *T. rex*. People say I have a knack for finding things and I do. I just open my eyes and look around and see what is there. In addition to being an underwater archaeological excavation diver, I am a field paleontologist. Every summer I go to the Badlands in the Dakotas and Wyoming to look for dinosaurs. I don't even pitch a tent. It's much nicer sleeping outside, looking at the stars—and if you're lucky, the aurora borealis. I just go. One summer in 1990, I was volunteering for Black Hills Institute, and we had excavated duckbill dinosaur bones for six weeks. And finally I had time toward the end of the summer to do some scouting on a neighboring ranch. The second to the last day of our season, (we were finishing excavating a triceratops skull) we woke up at the camp site and found we had a flat tire on the truck. I was so pleased as the rest of the team (Pete and Terry and two children, Matt, 10, and Jason, 16) went to the nearest town to fix the tire. My dog Gypsy and I had most of the day to finally go look at one small exposure of the Badlands that had been "calling" me for two weeks, but I hadn't had time to go there and look. Until the flat tire! It was a window of opportunity! Usually I just find scraps of bones. But I looked up and just saw her in the rocks. It was awesome. Once I found her I turned her over to the Institute. We excavated her, meaning we had the laborious task of cutting her out of the rock and carting her to the museum. But the preparators then had to spend years chipping away the rock around the fossilized bones, assembling the skeleton and studying her.

POLK: You are interested in and involved in such a diverse range of topics from underwater archaeology to dinosaurs to shells. What motivates you?

HENDRICKSON: Don't forget amber—though I'm not as actively seeking new specimens as in the past. It is still one of my main loves and expertise. Although I am a shy person, when something comes along that interests me, I lose my shyness. I want to learn everything I can about that subject. I identify the experts, find them and go pick their brains. I always go straight to the top. I don't want to waste time—I want to learn all I can and then go out in the field to see what I can discover. I am very persistent and an omnivore when I become interested in a particular subject.

POLK: What are you involved with now?

HENDRICKSON: I have been working on a book about conch pearls. It is a subject that has interested me since I was a young diver. I used to earn money by diving for shells off the Florida coast and selling them from my car along the Pacific coast. It paid for my cross country drive home to see my family in Seattle. I had heard about conch shell pearls then but I had never seen any. So all these years I have been looking for them. And I have been lucky enough to buy some wonderful ones from fishermen all over the Caribbean, which are now part of the traveling *Pearl* exhibit sponsored by the American Museum of Natural History and the Field Museum.

POLK: I understand you have started a scholarship program. Tell us about that.

HENDRICKSON: I think it is so imperative for all "lucky" people to take care of as many less fortunate people as possible. Years ago, I told my family not to buy me anything for Christmas. I wanted them to use their money and the money I would have spent on their presents to give to a Peruvian family I knew who had eight children. Now years later all but two of them have received university degrees. They just needed a little more help to move up from "poor" to middle class. If only each of us would help one poor family think what a difference we could make in people's lives.

POLK: Your home base is an island in Honduras. Why did you pick such a remote place?

HENDRICKSON: Honduras is my first and only home. For 30 years I never had a house, I was constantly traveling. I did not want to worry about paying rents and problems that often arise with owning a house. I did not want to be "tied" or anchored by the responsibility of a house or apartments. The pure freedom to go at a moment's notice has been extremely important to me and my life. I attribute many of my accomplishments just to the fact that I could go! I have successfully cut off the "tentacles" of normal life, and kept my freedom to choose what I would be doing. Then I bit the bullet and built a house.

D

I picked Honduras because it is remote. There are no cars where I am. My house is on the sea and there is great diving. It is like living on a boat, where I spent years, but it's great in storms! I don't have to go check the bilge to see if we're sinking! I can finally sleep all night!

POLK: What are your personal goals?

HENDRICKSON: Well I love diving and always will. I am involved in another site off the coast of Egypt in the Bay of Abou Qir where we have found shipwrecks from the time of Napoleon to antiquity And the sunken city of Herakleion, the port at the ancient entrance to the River Nile. This will keep me busy probably for the rest of my life. And I still want to return to Peru where I have hunted for fossil whales. I would like to go to Antarctica to look for dinosaur bones but it is so cold there that I might let that one go. I want to continue to build more museum exhibitions that make people say "wow". For example, I would like to find a wooly mammoth and put it in a giant, real ice cube so people could go up and touch it. There is technology that might make this possible. And I want to keep searching the Cuban waters for Cortez's ship that sank with all the treasure that was raised to pay Montezuma's ransom. The film *Pirates of the Caribbean* is partially based on that story combined with the true history of some real life pirates. I enjoyed the movie because they got most things archaeologically right, like the ship, the pirate's town, even the source of the treasure. Of course the ghosts and their story aren't true but the rest of it is wonderfully accurate.

POLK: What is the greatest challenge ahead for us?

HENDRICKSON: I am an optimist on the personal level but a pessimist on the larger scale. We humans can't control ourselves. We destroy everything. Sometimes I would like the dinosaurs to come back and eat everyone! We try to manage or control all the other species and make no real effort to control ourselves by overpopulating the planet. We have totally stressed the whole world. There is not enough of anything! To keep us going we are wiping out many species, some even before we know they exist. Our greatest challenge is to preserve the world. The oceans are so incredibly important and key for the future for our very survival. I believe that education, communication, and tolerance are important to help find solutions to our larger problems. Everyone needs to be educated about the repercussions of what we are doing. Most people don't have a clue why we are doing what we

E

do. We also need to allow people to be different and not impose our ways on them.

Proper communication from personal levels to inter-country levels could prevent needless warfares. We must attempt to evolve into humans who can resolve differences with communication and compromise.

POLK: What words of advice do you have for us?

HENDRICKSON: I wish all young adults could go spend 3 months or a year in a third world country so they could understand that 90 percent of the world does not live like [people in the first world] do. This is important in order to develop not only tolerance for other ways but to open their eyes and minds to a whole vast world outside what they are used to. The most important thing is for everyone to have an open mind, to be curious and follow your dreams. And if you don't have a dream now, don't worry. Just try a lot of different things and new ideas will keep emerging. To me, it isn't so much your level of intelligence or luck as it is your persistence. If you really want to do something, go for it. You must believe in yourself. You can do anything in spite of what anyone says.

You can be a spectator or you can be a doer participating and contributing. The choice is yours.

Sue, her sister Karen, her brother John, and her mother Mary walk along the beach in this family photo taken in Fort Lauderdale, Florida, where they often vacationed while visiting Sue's extended family. This was the trip that Sue began collecting beach shells (a task for which she employed the bag she holds in this photo), a hobby she continues to this day.

F

Hendrickson carries conch shells in either hand in this photo from her early days as an explorer. She had just begun collecting conch shells to clean and sell to shell collectors. During this time, she lived on this tug boat in Key West, performing salvage work and diving for lobster to earn a living. Though Hendrickson had recently dropped out of high school, she quickly learned to rely on her natural intelligence and skills to carve out the life that made her the happiest.

Sue stands between her beloved Uncle John Hendrickson on the left and her brother John Hendrickson on the right in this 1975 photo taken in Florida. Although Sue was living far away from her family, who first lived in Indiana and then Washington State, she managed to maintain her close familial ties while living independently in Florida.

Sue poses with a camel in Morocco in 1983. Hendrickson's activities in the African country included hunting for fossils, ammonites and tribolites, shark teeth, and mineral specimens.

Using a metal detector, Hendrickson hunts for meteorites in Chile. Metal detectors are helpful in this search as meteorites, matter that has fallen from outer space, typically have a metallic composition.

This scorpion trapped in amber is one of Hendrickson's finest pieces. She had originally tried to mine for amber herself, but quickly decided the work was too time consuming and began purchasing amber from other miners. Hendrickson has developed a positive reputation for her willingness to share her spectactular pieces with scientists.

Hendrickson poses with Pete Larson, his children Tim, Sarah, and Matt, as well as Terry Wentz and the elderly Ruth Mason, for whom the Ruth Mason Quarry, which Larson's Black Hills Institute explored, was named.

Hendrickson carefully labors to excavate Sue. Digging out a fossil is meticulous work: excavators must work slowly and deliberately, employing a wide range of tools and treating the fossil with great delicacy.

Hendrickson and Terry Wentz, the Black Hills Institute's chief preparator (standing left, next to Hendrickson), as well as other members of the BHI, pose with the partly-excavated skull of Sue. Because Sue's skull was packed so closely in the rock with her pelvis, the entire block of rock had to be moved to the lab where her skull and pelvis were carefully separated.

Terry Wentz, Hendrickson, and Peter Larson proudly stand in front of their famous *T. rex*, Sue. Wentz, Hendrickson, and Larson were the three main excavators of Sue, and although the Black Hills Institute ultimately did not maintain ownership of the fossil, the three excavators are still associated with the famous dinosaur.

Hendrickson kneels on a beach littered with conch shells. People collect conch shells for many reasons, including the beauty of the shells and the tasty conch meat. Hendrickson's favorite thing about conch shells is the lovely pink pearls she buys from the fisherman.

L

Diving with Carisub in Cuba, Hendrickson discovers artifacts from a shipwreck.

Hendrickson, Father Gabriel Casal, director of the Philippines National Museum, and Franck Goddio, director of the European Institute of Underwater Archaeology, marvel over the incredible collection of well preserved Ming porcelain they recovered from the *San Diego*, a shipwreck off the coast of the Philippines. The dive resulted in the collection of over 30,000 artifacts, from the Ming china to jewelry, shoe buckles, and bronze cannons.

M

Divers on one of Franck Goddio's many Egyptian expeditions bring an enormous ancient statue to the surface. Statues were not the only thing Goddio and his team discovered underwater in Egypt; they also found the sunken royal port of Alexandria, including the isle of Antirrhodos, huge slabs inscribed with hieroglyphics (known as stelae), and sphinxes from Cleopatra's own temple.

Hendrickson, her dog Skywalker, and Jean-Claude Roubaud, dive-master for Franck Goddio's team, provide a sense of the huge proportions of the statues they recovered from their dives in Egypt. In the foreground is the largest stela found in the world, circa 300 B.C., inscribed with three-quarter-inch hieroglyphics and quarter-inch Greek writing. Behind the stela are statues of a queen and the River Nile god Hapy, both circa 300 B.C. These artifacts were raised from the submeged city Herakleion.

Hendrickson and her dog Skywalker pose with Franck Goddio's team during one of their successful dives in Egypt. On the left stands a magnificent example of a stela inscribed with Egyptian hieroglyphics, while the statue in the middle is the ancient Egyptian goddess, Isis.

that the species were not just predators but rather "opportunistic [feeders]," who sometimes hunted but at other times scavenged.

Just a little over one year after Hendrickson discovered Sue, Larson was ready to tell his professional colleagues about her. He presented a slide show and a paper at the Fifty-First Annual Meeting of the Society of Vertebrate Paleontology (SVP) in October 1991. Like all presenters, he was given 12 minutes to speak. By this time, BHI's chief preparator, Terry Wentz, had been at work on Sue in the BHI lab for 12 months.

Wentz was still working on removing the skull from the pelvis. It was only after he finished this arduous task that he started to work on the other bones, a process that involved removing the plaster her bones had been covered with and taking off the foil underneath. Then he removed rock that surrounded her the bones, using an assortment of tools: an air scribe, which is like a tiny jackhammer; dental probes; brushes—first paintbrushes and then toothbrushes—and finally a Micro-airbrade, which blasted away the last remaining particles with baking soda. Next, Wentz repaired cracked bones with superglue. Finally, he applied putty in gaps in the bones. All along the way, he worked on identifying bones for the day when the skeleton would be assembled.[47] One of his most amazing finds were the tiny bones from Sue's hearing apparatus.[48]

Larson had had time not only to learn about Sue from Wentz and through his own observation but also to read up on—and visit, in some cases—the tyrannosaurs that had been discovered before Sue. Thus he spoke with authority as he discussed what he thought was "startling" about Sue. He described her tail and revealed that a duckbill skeleton had been found with her and that there was evidence (its bones were coated with ironstone) that the smaller animal, which had been found in her stomach, had been her last meal. He also talked about four bones, thought to come from three other tyrannosaurs, found in the vicinity and indicated that he believed there were 18 more months of work to be done on Sue. At the end of his talk, he extended an open invitation to Hill City to other paleontologists interested in inspecting the specimen.

Five months after the SVP meeting, on March 13, 1992, Peter Larson, Neal Larson, and Bob Farrar signed the papers necessary to create a nonprofit corporation. They had reached the point at which they were ready to begin fundraising for the museum they had been dreaming about. That same year, Larson made a shocking announcement: Sue was almost certainly female. Up to that point, many scientists had assumed that in the *T. rex* species, smaller "gracile" (graceful or slender) specimens were female and larger, "robust" specimens were male. Larson, however, argues to this day that this particular specimen was female. He speculates that she was in fact a matriarch, or a female head of a family.

Larson's thoughts had been focused on one particular study he wanted to do on Sue: He wanted to have a CAT scan done of her skull, which would involve running the skull through a special scanner that makes a series of photographs of microscopically thin segments of bone. (CAT scanners are generally found in hospitals, where doctors use them to diagnose and assess patients' ailments). Bob Bakker and Andrew Leitch, a paleontologist from Toronto, had negotiated on Larson's behalf with administrators at NASA, which had a huge, cutting-edge CAT scanner it used to look for flaws in space shuttle and rocket parts.

In April, BHI had another news announcement to make: It was about to begin work on excavating another new *T. rex* named Stan. This skeleton had been discovered on a ranch in the Badlands 90 miles west of Faith by an amateur named Stan Sacrison. Snow—only somewhat unusual for South Dakota in that part of the year—would hamper progress, but the BHI staff nevertheless was generally joyful and had good expectations. Then, suddenly, on April 29, they received the disturbing word that the Cheyenne River Sioux had gone to the press to claim ownership of Sue. The state's U.S. attorney was in the middle of an ongoing investigation into the matter. Larson's attorney assured him that the claim seemed ungrounded, and Larson returned to work on Stan and his plans for crating Sue's skull. At the same time, he was laying plans for a monograph—a scholarly book—on the *T. rex.* There already were plenty of books about dinosaurs in general, but he wanted to produce the first book devoted exclusively to the species. He had enlisted 34 specialists to make their own contributions, to write about whatever it was they were especially interested in. Larson hoped it would be just the beginning. Exhibitions, tours, casts of Sue and Stan shown together, allowing spectators to make their own comparisons—he came up with idea after idea. He fully expected that fame and academic recognition would come to him next. "It was time for us to burst into the mainstream," Larson later wrote in his own book about Sue.[49]

On May 13, they were very close to finishing construction of a special crate for the skull when Larson was visited by Stanley Robins, a National Park ranger with whom Larson had been acquainted for a long time (they met when they were both appointed to the state's State Historical Society Task Force on Paleontology). Larson, who always liked to demonstrate the awe he felt for Sue by showing off the work being done on her, took Robins back to the room where Wentz labored.

Although Larson did not know it at the time, that visit seems now to have been the beginning of his troubles. When Robins learned of Larson's plans, he reported to federal government officials that the skull was to be moved from BHI premises in a matter of days for the planned CAT scan at NASA. The FBI decided that the time had come to take action. At dawn the next day, they arrived at BHI with warrants in hand and seized Sue, claiming that she was not property of the Institute. The papers they showed Larson that day claimed that Sue belonged to the Sioux tribe, although later the warrant was amended to read that she belonged to the federal government. Despite vigorous protests not just on the part of the Larsons, Wentz, and the rest of BHI, but seemingly the entire population of Hill City, all of Sue's bones were crated up, loaded onto trailer trucks, and taken away to be stored at the South Dakota School of Mines. Everybody involved with Sue, including Hendrickson, was about to be embroiled in controversy. As months stretched into years, the investigation, and then the court cases concerning ownership and BHI's collecting practices, dragged on and on.

The fight over Sue made Hendrickson extremely unhappy. Even her involvement on the edge of the fight left her stressed and even more distrustful of her fellow human beings. Hendrickson says that she felt complete disbelief as she came to realize that, in regard to Sue, the United States judicial system was being manipulated by just a few people.[50]

Hendrickson was in France the morning the FBI went to BHI to take away her namesake. She learned by telephone that Sue's ownership was in dispute and that the FBI moved Sue into storage at the School of Mines and Technology, into a steel tank in a machine shop. Larson, Wentz, Hendrickson, and plenty of others were especially unhappy with these arrangements because part of Sue's mineral content was pyrite, which meant that if she was not kept in a rigorously controlled environment, her skeleton might be ruined.

Despite a series of desperate attempts on the part of BHI to free Sue, she stayed imprisoned until a whole series of court cases ended. Hearings seemed to go on and on, and Hendrickson was an unhappy witness. She had to give testimony concerning how Sue was found and about the deal between Larson and Maurice Williams. She was also asked questions about Larson's collecting habits, some of them probing into actions he had taken years ago, when they had collaborated with Kirby Siber on a whale dig in Peru.

Finally, in 1997, the last trial came to a close. When the judge put down his gavel, he ruled that Williams was Sue's rightful owner. This was bad enough for Larson and his friends, but the situation became even worse when the Larson brothers were brought to trial on 153 criminal counts, including allegedly removing other fossils from government land, as well as money laundering and illegal purchasing overseas. In the long run, they were both found guilty, but only on a handful of counts between the two of them. Neal Larson received a probated sentence for a misdemeanor—he had removed fossils that were valued at less than $100 from the Buffalo Gap National Grasslands (he had testified that when he found the fossils he thought he was on land belonging to a local grazing association). BHI as an entity was found guilty on four felony counts, which involved three customs violations and one instance of accepting a catfish fossil that had been found in Badlands National Park from a collector. It would be fined. Bob Farrar was convicted on two felony counts of undervaluing fossils at customs checkpoints. Like his brother, Peter Larson was found guilty of having stolen fossils from the Buffalo Gap Grasslands. He was also convicted of failing to declare a large sum in traveler's checks on a trip from Japan back to the United States and failing to report cash he carried on another collecting trip to Peru. He was sentenced to two years at a federal minimum security facility.[51]

Far from settled was whether federal lands would be open to fossil hunters in the future. There remained an enormous amount of animosity between those involved in commercial concerns and a few members of the academic community.

Once judged the sole owner of Sue, Maurice Williams decided to sell her. He entertained offers from at least three museums, but he held out, wanting to make as much money as possible from his prize. An executive at Sotheby's, one of the world's most famous auction houses, became interested in the story and approached Williams to ask him to let them sell

Sue on his behalf. Williams agreed to the deal, telling a reporter he hoped to reap a half-million dollars from the sale of Sue. On November 16, 1996, science writer Malcolm W. Browne reported in *The New York Times* that Sue might be expected to go for more than one million dollars, which would break the record, making her the most expensive fossil ever.

The many crates that held Sue were shipped to the auction house in New York City, where the bones were inventoried, photographed, and cataloged. The news that Sue would be sold to the highest bidder created another media frenzy. American paleontologists expressed concern that a private collector or a foreign museum might pay the most for her. This would make her unavailable for them to study. To try to prevent this from happening, Sotheby's announced that it would offer any *American* institution the option of paying off the specimen over time and it would forego interest.

As the day approached and Sotheby's registered bidders, a few private individuals declared their intention to bid. Museums with funds also registered. They wanted her for the scientific information she would yield and her potential to draw grant money and generate commercial income. Everybody understood that owning Sue would bring thousands upon thousands of visitors to a museum and create an awesome reputation.

While Sue was at Sotheby's, paleontologists came to admire her. In May 1997, *Nature* magazine published an article announcing that the dinosaur had suffered from gout because she had crystal deposits in the joints in her metacarpals (the bones in her "hands"), which would have caused her horrible pain. This information was based on a bone disease specialist's study of a cast that paleontologist Ken Carpenter had had made of the forelimb when Sue was still in Larson's hands.[52] Another study, this one of her facial bones, showed that she had on more than one occasion suffered from deep gashes. One fight had left another dinosaur's tooth stuck in one of her ribs.

In September, Sotheby's opened a Sue exhibit in its gallery in downtown New York. At that time, almost all of the bones remained in their original field jackets. Crowds, including excited groups of schoolchildren and a group of Japanese videographers, flocked to see Sue's huge skull and her scary claws.

As the day approached, the sale got a lot of coverage in the press. Unfortunately, the hype surrounding the auction seemed to have some negative outcomes. In Montana, for example, Dr. Keith Rigby and a group of students had spent most of the summer working on a dinosaur dig. As the season ended, they had to stop working and leave the site despite the fact that they had not finished their excavation. When Rigby got a phone call at the university reporting that vandals were digging up the specimen he and his students had been working on, he blamed Sotheby's, saying that news of the auction had made people greedy for fossils and the money they could generate.

In the article that appeared in *The New York Times* the day before Sue went on the auction block, Malcolm Browne predicted that the auction would be attended by "federal agents, museum curators, Indian tribal leaders, paleontologists, university representatives, commercial fossil dealers, academic paleontologists and people with no special qualifications apart from a fascination with dinosaurs."[53] He pointed out that although *T. rex* teeth and bone fragments had been sold before, this would be the first sale at auction of an entire tyrannosaur skeleton.[54] A Sotheby's representative stated that the sale might take just three minutes.[55]

On the morning of October 4, a long line of excited people snaked along a wall on Manhattan's York Avenue, waiting for the doors of Sotheby's to open. When the time finally came, 300 people rushed in, filling the auction room virtually to capacity. Sue Hendrickson came to the auction, hoping that the sale would result in BHI getting Sue back:

South Dakota businessman Stanford M. Adelstein was there on BHI's behalf. He had promised that if he won Sue, he would give her back to Larson so that the people of his state could realize their dream of having a dinosaur museum. A total of nine people had registered to bid. Some of them sat in chairs on the auction house floor. Others hid from sight in Sotheby's "skyboxes." Sotheby's staff members also took some bids over the telephone.

From the moment the bidding began at just after 10:00 A.M., it was "rapid-fire," in the words of one journalist.[56] Bidding started at a half-million dollars and had soon reached 3, 4, and 5 million dollars. When it reached $5.2 million, the man representing the Field Museum of Chicago entered his first bid: $5.9 million. By the time the bidding reached $7 million, action had slowed considerably. Most bidders had reached their absolute limit. Still, four more bids came in: $7.1 million, $7.2 million, $7.5 million. At a signal from the Field's skybox, the auctioneer announced $7.6 million. A moment of silence followed. He said the number again. Still silence. "Fair warning," he stated, declaring Sue going, going . . . Then she was gone. When the gavel went down, the room went wild. In the end, the Field Museum paid $8.36 million for Sue (the final selling price of the fossil plus Sotheby's standard commission of 10 percent).

Within moments, two of the Field's highest administrators and the professional bidder they had hired were at Sotheby's podium. Everybody wanted to know who they were. Richard Gray, who bid on behalf of the museum, read a prepared statement beginning, "This morning I have the pleasure of having been awarded custody of Sue, the world's largest and probably oldest young lady. She will spend her next birthday—that's her 70 millionth [actually she was 65 or 66 million years old]—in her new home on the shores of Lake Michigan. This is, of course, in Chicago at the renowned Field Museum of Natural History."[57] The Field itself had not had enough money in

After an extensive legal battle, Maurice Williams was awarded sole ownership of the *T. rex* Sue, which was discovered on his property. The esteemed Sotheby's auction house persuaded Williams to allow the *T. rex* to be sold by them. On October 4, 1997, the day of the auction, Sotheby's was packed with spectators, journalists, and potential buyers. Although the competition to win Sue was intense, the Chicago Field Museum ultimately acquired the fossil for $8.36 million with funds donated by McDonald's and Disney.

its coffers to make such a huge bid, but it had the promise of a huge contribution from McDonald's. The Walt Disney Corporation and some private donors also agreed to help pay for the purchase.

Hendrickson expressed satisfaction with the outcome. Of course she would have liked to see Sue go back to BHI, but the Field is one of the world's finest natural history museums. She knew that the Field would hire the best staff to study Sue and display her to full advantage. On October 20, 1997, Sue arrived at the Field in boxes. Eager to show her off, the museum mounted a temporary exhibition built around her that began in November. When the show closed after the holidays in January 1998, Sue went back behind closed doors for preparation and mounting. The museum, lacking a dinosaur paleontologist, launched a head hunt to look for a young postgraduate. Chris Brochu, a crocodile specialist, was chosen for the job of chief scientist, despite the fact that he had yet to celebrate his thirtieth birthday.

The Field hired preparators to begin the three-year-long process of cleaning and stabilizing the bones. The Field also hired Philip Fraley to undertake the separate task of Sue's mounting. Fraley, who already had an enviable position at the American Museum of Natural History, quit his job and opened his own restoration business so that he could work on her. McDonald's paid for a special lab to be built upstairs at the museum. A second lab was built for further preparation of Sue at Disney's DinoLand USA. Each lab featured huge plate-glass windows through which visitors could watch the work being done on her. Both proved to be big tourist attractions.

When Sue got to the Field, more than half of her bones had yet to be pried from the rock that had encased them for 65 million years. The staff had to chip and abrade the rock. As each new bone was released, it was studied. Some of what Brochu saw dovetailed with earlier reports. In other cases, what he discovered led him to draw his own conclusions— or, in cases, in which he was not sure what he was looking at, reserve judgment. For example, in one place on the jawbone there was a series of holes. Earlier researchers thought that they were tooth marks. Detailed study caused Brochu to suggest another possibility: that at one point in her life, Sue had a wound there that became infected and failed to heal well, leaving her scarred.[58]

Brochu made arrangements for a CAT scan—as Peter Larson had wanted—at a Boeing lab in California.[59] Viewing the scan on his computer screen, the series of X rays let him look at the inside of the skull a fraction of an inch at a time. Among the amazing things he discovered is the actual size of Sue's brain. Despite the fact that Sue was an enormous animal weighing about seven tons, the space in her skull for her brain—the braincase—is so small it would hold just one quart of milk. On the other hand, Brochu discovered that she had larger olfactory bulbs than he expected. Each of the two bulbs is larger than her cerebrum, which means Sue had an extremely keen sense of smell.[60]

While Brochu finished his preliminary study of Sue, and the preparators finished cleaning her bones, Fraley began working on her. In March 1999, the Field sent Sue's bones to a foundry (a place where metal is cast) in New Jersey. Having put her back together—the process was like working on a jigsaw puzzle—Fraley and the Field Museum worked out how she might best be displayed. They realized that the skull was too heavy to be attached, so it was replaced by a realistic lightweight cast. A separate display was built around the genuine skull. One by one, they designed and created the steel framework that today holds Sue's bones together for display. The most amazing thing about Fraley's mounting is that it allows the removal of just one bone—any bone—for study. The bones are not actually permanently attached in any way.[61]

On May 17, 2000, the Field Museum opened its permanent exhibition of Sue. Thousands of people packed the museum for the unveiling of Sue, waiting anxiously for the huge curtain covering Sue to drop and reveal the skeleton in all its glory. Hendrickson and her dog Skywalker (Gypsy's grandniece), invited as guests of honor, were photographed by the skeleton, glowing with happiness. Although she remained uncomfortable in the spotlight, Hendrickson succumbed to the demands of the public, even appearing on one of the morning news programs broadcast nationally. The next day, newspapers around the world ran articles about the exhibit on their front pages.

Sue was mounted by Philip Fraley and his talented team of fossil preparators, who pose with Hendrickson in this photo. Fraley, standing on the left in the back, left his position at the American Museum of Natural History in order to work on Sue. Fraley mounted Sue in such a way that any bone can be removed for study without disturbing the rest of the skeleton.

From that point on, Sue made virtually every list of Chicago's top attractions. She has fulfilled all of the Field administration's hopes and continues to draw visitors, including tourists and scholars, to the museum. Thanks to the support from McDonald's, however, people do not necessarily have to travel to Chicago to see Sue. Three life-size casts have been made of the skeleton. One is on permanent display at DinoLand USA in Disneyworld. The other two casts are part of traveling exhibits, which, along with books, articles, and websites about Sue, ensures that people who do not live in or travel to Chicago can also marvel over her.

7

Hendrickson
After Sue
1992–2004

Sue Hendrickson will always feel a deep personal attachment to her namesake. After all, she is the one to whom Sue "called." Nevertheless, Hendrickson has had in many ways only a fleeting relationship with the *T. rex*. Although Hendrickson stayed in South Dakota long enough to help find and excavate Sue's skeleton, she left only three weeks after her discovery. Reading accounts of the Sue saga, one might well get the impression that Hendrickson fled the scene.[62] When she left, however, she had no idea that there would be a media frenzy over Sue. Hendrickson was simply heading back to work in her other major field of interest, marine archaeology.

Hendrickson's first attempt to take part in an underwater archaeology expedition may have been a bust (the team with which she first went to the Dominican Republic never did get the permit they needed to search for a Spanish galleon), but in the years that followed, she gained considerable experience as a marine archaeologist while working as a diver for a variety of people.

The Dominican Republic was just one place she enjoyed diving. Another was Cuba, the Communist island nation located 100 miles south of the tip of Florida. Hendrickson first went to Cuba for sailboat racing in the late 1970s. In Florida, she and a boyfriend had been asked to do sea trials on one of the first J24s—among the fastest, sleekest sailboats ever made—off the assembly line. She would spend two years on teams, racing J24s as well as bigger sailboats. Because she was the only woman on board, a lot of grunt work fell to her, yet for a long time she loved the thrill of racing. From the 1930s until 1960, there was an annual race from St. Petersburg, on the southwestern side of Florida, to Havana, Cuba. When relations between the United States and Cuba fell apart during the Cuban Missile Crisis era, the race was cancelled. During President Jimmy Carter's administration, tensions between the two nations eased enough for the race to be held once more, and Hendrickson was one of the organizers. While in Key West, she formed what would become a lifelong friendship with Vicente de la Guardia, the Cuban government liaison who was in charge of all water sports in Cuba.

De la Guardia, who had lived in the United States while attending Duke University, was an expert sailor and diver. As director of Carisub—a Cuban team of marine archaeologists sponsored by the government-controlled company Cimex—he was in charge of some exciting ventures, including exploring Spanish and other Colonial ships that sank off the coast of Cuba when Spain was expanding its influence in the New World.

Eventually, Hendrickson became a liaison for Carisub. Cuba, typically isolated from the rest of the West because it is a Communist country, needed help keeping up with advances made in the field. Hendrickson helped them contact marine archaeologists in other locations by sponsoring Carisub members' trips to the annual meetings held by historical archaeologists. She also helped them get copies of publications they needed. In 1991, de la Guardia asked her to find a foreign group that could provide Carisub with the equipment they lacked, such as high-tech magnetometers (an instrument that detects metallic substances or the intensity of magnetic fields) and sonars. While looking for a group that might be interested in cooperating with Carisub, Hendrickson met Franck Goddio, "probably the most successful marine archaeologist in the world."[63] Born in France, Goddio was a financial consultant before becoming involved in underwater archaeology in Asia. Five years earlier, he had founded the Institut Européen d'Archéologie de Sous-Marine. Goddio responded to Hendrickson's invitation by going to Cuba to meet with Carisub, with whom he would begin work on a long-standing cooperative project, searching for wrecks with de la Guardia, Hendrickson, and others.

Hendrickson's work as a liaison to Carisub ended after Carisub came under control of the Cuban navy. By that time, however, she had begun to work with Goddio on a regular basis.

The mariner's astrolabes these Carisub members (Xavier Hermès, Franck Goddio, and Nelson Garcia, Jr.) hold were used in the fifteenth and sixteenth centuries by sailors to determine the latitude of their ship by measuring the noon altitude of the sun. Hendrickson became a liaison for Carisub, a team of marine archaeologists sponsored by the Cuban government, helping them connect with other marine archaeologists in the field and even joining them on dives.

As time went by, she would be part of the crew on several of his biggest projects.

In 1991, Goddio and his team located the wreck of the *San Diego,* a Spanish galleon that sank off the Philippines more than 400 years ago, in the days when trade flourished and ships sailed constantly back and forth between two far-flung Spanish outposts, Mexico and the Philippines.[64] Spain's biggest rival at the time was the Netherlands, now a small nation but then a powerhouse that, like Spain, was seeking to build a worldwide empire. The Netherlands sent out a small fleet to the Philippines, and, seeking to prevent Spanish ships from entering, posted one small ship, the *Mauritius,* outside Manila Bay.

When the *San Diego* came into view, the *Mauritius* prepared for battle. The Spanish captain's account claimed that when he found his ship under attack, he ordered his crew of 350 to get ready to fight. After ramming the *Mauritius,* the *San Diego* maintained its position alongside the Dutch ship. Yelling what translates into English as "Surrender, dogs!", armored Spanish soldiers tied the two ships together. They put planks down between the ships and surged onto their enemy's craft. A Spanish victory seemed certain.

It was not to be. The *San Diego*, overloaded with cargo, sat so far down in the water that her gunports were below the waterline. None of her cannons could be fired, and she started to leak. When the Dutch crew had given up and were hiding belowdecks, their captain set his own ship on fire to force them back on deck and fight. Fearing that his own vessel would catch on fire, the captain of the Spanish ship, Lieutenant Governor Antonio de Morga, ordered his men to cut the ships loose. Being tied to the *Mauritus* had kept the overloaded *San Diego* afloat; when the ties were severed, the "sea devoured [the *San Diego*] in one fatall morsell," wrote a seventeenth-century chronicler. [65] Only 100 survived of the 500 men onboard.

Goddio's dive team had deliberately been searching for this wreck. Having read the contemporary accounts of the sinking and studied the nautical charts, they hazarded an educated guess as to where to look and then used a magnetometer to search for the *San Diego*. They located it 175 feet below sea level. When Hendrickson joined the crew in 1992, they brought in water dredges to remove the sand and sediment that covered the ship. An extra-strong double pump helped them remove tons of rock that the ship had been carrying as ballast, which took a month of solid labor. It proved well worth the effort: Underneath the rocks, they found a nearly perfectly preserved hull and keel.

Ultimately, the expedition yielded parts of skeletons of 100 crewmen and almost 30,000 artifacts, including an incredible

Divers working under the direction of Franck Goddio carefully label and explore the shipwrecked *San Diego* 175 feet below sea level. The Spanish ship, which had sunk during a battle with the Dutch off the coast of the Philippines in 1600, yielded almost 30,000 artifacts, including a collection of Chinese porcelain. Hendrickson described the ship as "by far the most complete shipwreck I have ever seen or hope to see from that time period."

collection of Ming porcelain from China as well as ceramics from six other countries! The ship would have disintegrated immediately if it were brought to the surface, but the artifacts were able to be recovered after underwater photographers and a robot capable of taking underwater images recorded the wreck for further study. As a result, there are video images accurate to within one centimeter of error that can be used to estimate the dimensions of the ship and where all the cargo was stored.

Hendrickson describes herself as feeling extremely lucky to have worked on this project in particular, saying, "It is by far the most complete shipwreck I have ever seen or hope to see from that time period."[66] She particularly likes to talk about the personal effects she found on the *San Diego,* such as shoe buckles, chess pieces, and a few pieces of jewelry, artifacts that help her imagine the very real lives that were lost. The *San Diego* is still considered the most famous underwater discovery in the Philippines. Today it is the subject of two permanent displays. Responding to a request from the king of Spain, Goddio sent a huge number of artifacts to the Museo Naval in Madrid. The National Museum of the Philippines has its own exhibit. In addition, there was a traveling exhibit that went to New York, Berlin, Madrid, and Paris, where a full-scale mock-up of the *San Diego* was mounted.

Hendrickson was also a member of one of Goddio's dive teams that explored the waters around Egypt. One of the sites they searched for, the Isle of Antirrhodos, is known from the history of Strabo, a Greek geographer and historian who lived during the time of Jesus Christ. According to Strabo, Antirrhodos is the island on which the Egyptian queen Cleopatra spent summers until her death in 30 B.C. Today, the site is the centerpiece of Project Alexandria, a huge undertaking that will hopefully result in an underwater museum where visitors can learn about the history of the most civilized city on earth 2,000 years ago.

Historians knew that Antirrhodos was submerged in a flood when an earthquake devastated the northern coast of Africa in approximately A.D. 400. In what the Discovery Channel described as "an amazing high-tech search," Goddio's team used the latest technology to locate the site.[67] They continue to find amazing artifacts on their annual dives, including items such two sphinxes—statues that guarded the entrance to Cleopatra's private temple that the queen herself had commissioned. They have also found and mapped the complete royal port located on the eastern edge of the harbor, the docks where Mark Antony lived, the Timonium, Cleopatra's palace,

As part of Franck Goddio's team, Sue Hendrickson explored the waters around Egypt, finding entire sunken cities as well as artifacts from sphinxes that guarded Cleopatra's temple to enormous stelae inscribed with hieroglyphics. This statue, Hapy, is the god of the River Nile. The statue, dating from 300 B.C., was found on the submerged city Herakleion.

another large temple, and two shipwrecks. In the sunken city of Menouthis, they located a temple measuring 492 feet long, as well as a marble panel featuring an elaborate carved cobra, numerous sphinxes, and other statues.

Also off the coast of Africa, one dive yielded a treasure trove from an entirely different era. Hendrickson was part of the Goddio team that located and began the long process of excavating two ships that belonged to a fleet of warships that Napoleon, emperor of France, lost in the naval Battle of the Nile in 1798. The most historically significant of those finds was *L'Orient,* one of Napoleon's best ships, sunk by British Admiral Horatio Nelson in the fight that caused Napoleon to abandon his attempt to take over Egypt.

In 2001, still with Goddio, Hendrickson was one of the marine archaeologists who discovered Herakleion—the city of Hercules—which was the ancient Egyptian port located at the entrance to the Nile River. That city sank underwater during an earthquake around 300 B.C. So far, swimming among ruined buildings and in and out of 13 shipwrecks, Goddio's team has found three 18-feet-tall statues of a pharaoh, a queen, and the

HENDRICKSON'S HISTORICAL TREASURES

As unbelievable as it may seem, Sue Hendrickson has made other discoveries as fascinating as Sue. The list of the historical treasures she has uncovered or helped uncover is a long one and includes:

- Prehistoric butterflies preserved in amber (Hendrickson once owned three of the only six ever located but has since sold or donated them all to museums)
- A fossil saber-toothed tiger
- Sue
- The *San Diego,* a seventeenth-century sunken Spanish galleon, the most significant marine archaeological find in the Philippines in many years
- A Chinese shipwreck from around the year 1500
- The submerged royal port and quarters of ancient Alexandria, Egypt
- French emperor Napoleon's flagship, *L'Orient,* lost in a sea battle in 1798

god of the River Nile. Hundreds of anchors and two stelae (large pillars or slabs used for commemoration), one small and one large—in fact the world's largest—have also been recovered. The latter bears inscriptions in both hieroglyphics and Greek.

To this day, Hendrickson works for Goddio as much as possible. Currently, Hendrickson hopes that as part of Goddio's team, she will be one of the people to discover Spanish conquistador Hernando Cortés's long-lost ship, which sank off Cuba in 1521.[68]

She continues to pursue other interests as well. For years, she had no permanent address. Around 1993, however, she decided the time finally had come for her to build her own house, a place to which she could return when she tired of globetrotting. For its location, she chose a small island off the coast of Honduras, in Central America, a quiet place of extraordinary natural beauty, with a coral reef within an easy swim.[69] Her home was just built when Honduras was devastated by Hurricane Mitch in 1998, Hendrickson devoted a tremendous amount of her time and large amounts of her own money to helping her neighbors rebuild and get back on their feet.

Today, she goes there for a couple of weeks at a time every three months or so. When she leaves, her caretaker and his family maintain her house and care for her many animals. Two or three times a year she goes to the Pacific Northwest to see her family (her mother is now approaching her eighty-seventh birthday). She still makes solitary trips out West, too, taking a couple of weeks or months whenever she can to explore more of the Badlands with her dog, Skywalker, the golden retriever she has had ever since Gypsy's death in 1994.

For years, Hendrickson has suffered from a disease that affects her lymph system. She has what is sometimes called elephantiasis, a swelling of a limb (in her case, one of her legs swells a great deal). Although she can move around freely, she will always have to see doctors and do physical therapy to be able to remain active. Still, on she goes.

8

Hendrickson's Influence

Sue Hendrickson acts so matter-of-fact when she describes herself as an explorer that one might wonder if she knows how remarkable it seems to most people to be an explorer in the twenty-first century. In an age in which many have concluded that there are no new frontiers (except in outer space, of course), Hendrickson continues to find new places to go on Earth, including many under sea.

Though Hendrickson has lived a largely nomadic life, constantly moving from place to place, she recently built a beautiful home in Honduras to return to in between projects. It is a place friends and family, and many pets, can enjoy, just as Sue's mother Mary, Sue, and her many dogs are in this photo taken of Sue's porch.

Today Hendrickson is regarded as an expert in several different fields. Summing up her own underwater accomplishments, she says she excels at diving and is an expert in marine archaeology, salvage work, and certain types of fishing. No one has more knowledge than she does of conch pearls—a very rare type of natural pearl. In terms of field paleontology, she has attained stature as an expert in fossil inclusions in amber.

Museum administrators and curators, university professors, field experts, and amateur naturalists all over the world express an absolute and well-founded respect for her. A curator at the American Museum of Natural History—

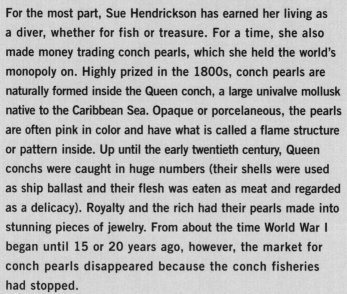

CONCH PEARLS

For the most part, Sue Hendrickson has earned her living as a diver, whether for fish or treasure. For a time, she also made money trading conch pearls, which she held the world's monopoly on. Highly prized in the 1800s, conch pearls are naturally formed inside the Queen conch, a large univalve mollusk native to the Caribbean Sea. Opaque or porcelaneous, the pearls are often pink in color and have what is called a flame structure or pattern inside. Up until the early twentieth century, Queen conchs were caught in huge numbers (their shells were used as ship ballast and their flesh was eaten as meat and regarded as a delicacy). Royalty and the rich had their pearls made into stunning pieces of jewelry. From about the time World War I began until 15 or 20 years ago, however, the market for conch pearls disappeared because the conch fisheries had stopped.

In the years during which she collected shells to sell, Hendrickson cleaned thousands of conchs and never found a single pearl. Then, one day, she was in the Bahamas, talking to a conch fisherman, and when she inquired about conch where she has made important contributions to the museum's collections and exhibitions of amber and pearls—describes her as "invaluable." [70] Colleagues in paleontology, including the world-famous Jack Horner, express admiration for her knowledge and an envy of her amazing ability to find lost treasures. Horner thinks that a combination of factors have contributed her ability: training, education, a trust in her own instinct, and a "keen eye." [71] Robert Bakker, another key figure in the world of paleontology, admires her adventuresome spirit and has described her as "a combination of Indiana Jones and John the Baptist—people who thrive in the wilderness." He says that her "calling" is the hunt—

pearls, he gave her one in trade. From that point on, she started to build a collection until she had enough of the stunningly beautiful pearls to show to dealers. It was Ryo Yamaguchi, an executive at Mikimoto Pearls in Japan, who first agreed with her that there could be a market for them. In the ten years before he retired from Mikimoto, Yamaguchi created a special line of conch jewelry every year. In 1987, conch pearls caught the eyes of the world when actress Liz Taylor was photographed wearing earrings and a necklace made of conch pearls by jeweler-to-the-stars Harry Winston.

For a while, Hendrickson devoted part of her time and energy to her conch pearl business. She employed buyers in 12 different countries. As the Queen conch became endangered (it has been overfished and its natural habitat is in danger), however, more and more nations prohibited conch fishing. Today, Hendrickson still remains very interested in the pearls— she is in the process of helping write a book about them and has donated stunning examples to several different museums— but her business no longer flourishes.

whether on land or under the water.[72] Franck Goddio and other marine archaeologists likewise express admiration for her abilities and comment in particular on how many of the recent great finds she has been in on.

It is not just her colleagues who find Hendrickson interesting and admirable. In 1999, she was asked to participate on the President's Panel for Ocean Exploration. As a member of the panel, she worked on several different agendas to help decide how the U.S. government could better explore the oceans. Hendrickson was frequently in the media limelight, especially during the period in which the Field unveiled Sue and she was featured in magazines and on news programs. Today, she says, she continues to get many telephone calls asking her for interviews or to make public appearances. (She still declines almost all requests, preferring to keep her life as private as possible. Reluctant to give speeches, she will however sometimes agree to do question-and-answer sessions, especially for children.) Thanks to women's studies scholars, her name now appears on lists of the most notable women of the twentieth century. Hendrickson was also profiled in a book about noteworthy women over 50 years of age, and in an essay in Milbry Polk and Mary Tiegreen's book on female explorers, *Women of Discovery: A Celebration of Intrepid Women Who Explored the World.*

Sue Hendrickson, a high school dropout, has been recognized twice by prestigious universities. The University of Illinois awarded Hendrickson an honorary doctorate in the year 2000 to the immense satisfaction of her mother, who always hoped that her middle child would one day go to college. In 2001, Barnard College also honored Hendrickson, selecting her as a recipient of its Medal of Distinction.[73] All of this pleases Hendrickson, of course, but what she really appreciates is the interest children show in her work. When it is brought to her attention, she seems surprised to learn that kids in general and girls in particular see her as a role model. When asked for advice, however, she brims over, encouraging everybody to join in her hunt, to go out into the world to search for the interesting and the new.

Chronology

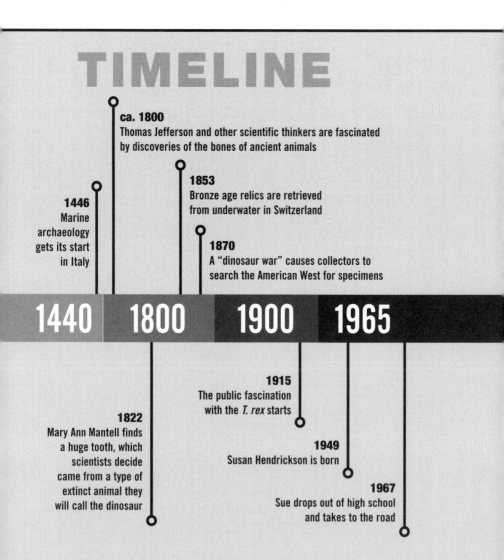

TIMELINE

ca. 1800
Thomas Jefferson and other scientific thinkers are fascinated by discoveries of the bones of ancient animals

1853
Bronze age relics are retrieved from underwater in Switzerland

1446
Marine archaeology gets its start in Italy

1870
A "dinosaur war" causes collectors to search the American West for specimens

1440   1800   1900   1965

1915
The public fascination with the *T. rex* starts

1822
Mary Ann Mantell finds a huge tooth, which scientists decide came from a type of extinct animal they will call the dinosaur

1949
Susan Hendrickson is born

1967
Sue drops out of high school and takes to the road

a sailboat. Hendrickson lives on the boat in a California marina, and from this point on, her life will revolve for many years around the water.

1973 Hendrickson is asked to participate in an underwater salvage project for the first time. In the years that follow, she will take part in many salvage projects, helping to bring up boats and planes from the bottom of the ocean.

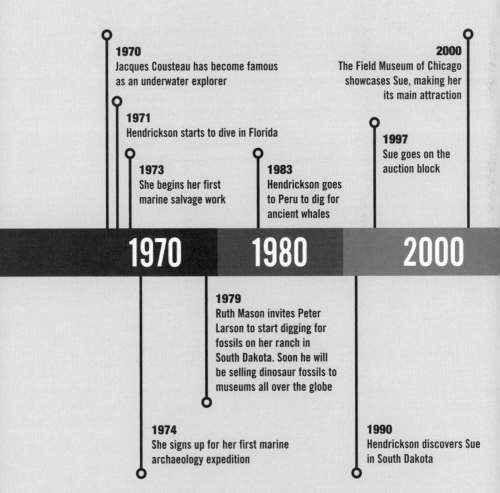

1970
Jacques Cousteau has become famous as an underwater explorer

2000
The Field Museum of Chicago showcases Sue, making her its main attraction

1971
Hendrickson starts to dive in Florida

1997
Sue goes on the auction block

1973
She begins her first marine salvage work

1983
Hendrickson goes to Peru to dig for ancient whales

1970   1980   2000

1979
Ruth Mason invites Peter Larson to start digging for fossils on her ranch in South Dakota. Soon he will be selling dinosaur fossils to museums all over the globe

1974
She signs up for her first marine archaeology expedition

1990
Hendrickson discovers Sue in South Dakota

Chronology

1974 Hendrickson decides to go on her first underwater archaeological expedition to the Dominican Republic. While in the Dominican Republic, she develops an interest in collecting amber.

1983 Hendrickson participates in a dig for fossils with Kirby Siber in an ancient Peruvian seabed, where she meets Peter Larson of the Black Hills Institute for the first time.

1989 Having been diagnosed with cervical cancer, Hendrickson undergoes surgery and is cured of the disease.

1990 During an excavation project in the Badlands, Sue Hendrickson goes on a walk and finds what will prove to be the world's largest and most complete *T. rex* skeleton on August 12.

1991 Hendrickson joins Franck Goddio's dive team and takes part in an amazing historic discovery of the wreck of the *San Diego*, a Spanish galleon which sailed at the very end of the sixteenth century.

1992 Dispute arises over the ownership of Sue. In May, FBI agents arrive at the Black Hills Institute with a warrant to seize the skeleton. In the years that follow, Peter Larson, as well as others, will be arrested and put on trial for charges relating to collecting of dinosaurs and other specimens.

1997 Following a judge's ruling that Maurice Williams is the rightful owner of Sue, Sotheby's, acting on Williams' behalf, auctions her off to the highest bidder. The Field Museum of Chicago ultimately wins the *T. rex*. By this time, Hendrickson divides her time diving off the coast of Egypt, visiting her family in the Seattle area, and trips to a house she has built in Honduras.

2000   The Field Museum opens its permanent Sue exhibit. Hendrickson is invited to attend as a guest of honor.

Notes

1. Black Hills Institute of Geological Research website at *http://www.bhigr.com/*.

2. Sue Hendrickson, *Hunt for the Past: My Life as an Explorer.* New York: Cartwheel Books, 2001, p. 7

3. Peter Larson and Kristin Donnan, *Rex Appeal.* Montpelier, VT: Invisible Cities Press, 2002, p. 8

4. This story has been retold in many different sources, including Hendrickson, *Hunt for the Past,* pp. 25–27; Steve Fiffer, *Tyrannosaurus Sue: The Extraordinary Saga of the Largest, Most Fought Over T-Rex Ever Found.* New York: W. H. Freeman & Co., 2000, pp. 19–20; and Larson and Donnan, pp. 6–12.

5. "BHI finds 4th T. Rex!," posted on the Archives of the DINOSAUR Mailing List, Cleveland Museum of Natural History website, *http://www.cmnh.org/dinoarch/1994Sep/msg00095.html.*

6. Memo from Sue Hendrickson to author, September 27, 2003.

7. Bruce Frankel, "The Bone Collector," *People,* July 24, 2000, pp. 129ff.

8. Frankel, "Bone Collector," p. 2.

9. Fiffer, *Tyrannosaurus Sue,* p. 22.

10. Hendrickson, *Hunt for the Past,* p. 28

11. Sue at the Field Museum, Sue's Vital Statistics, Field Museum web page at *http://www.fmnh.org/sue/vital.html,* copyright 2003.

12. Memo from Hendrickson to author, September 27, 2003.

13. Neal Larson, "The Story of a Dinosaur Named Sue, Part 2— Discovery and Excavation," Black Hills Institute of Geological Research website at *http://www.bhigr.com/pages/info/info_sue_2.htm.*

14. Fiffer, *Tyrannosaurus Sue,* p. 25.

15. Ibid., p. 37–38.

16. Memo from Hendrickson to author, September 27, 2003.

17. Fiffer, *Tyrannosaurus Sue,* p. 43.

18. Malcolm W. Browne, "Fetching T. Rex Fossil May Fetch $1 Million Plus, Experts Say," *New York Times,* November 16, 1996.

19. Ibid.

20. Malcolm W. Browne, "Tyrannosaur Skeleton is Sold to a Museum for $8.36 Million," *New York Times,* October 5, 1997.

21. Kathy Passero, "Sue Hendrickson, A Real-Life Indiana Jones," *Biography,* November 2000, p. 4.

22. Memo from Hendrickson to author, September 27, 2003.

23. Ibid.

24. Sue Hendrickson, interview with author, July 2003.

25. Ibid.

26. Hendrickson, *Hunt for the Past,* p. 6.

27. Ibid., p. 9

28. Steve Brusatte, "What About the Susan Who Found Sue: A Portrait of Susan Hendrickson," *Paleozoica, http://www.dinodata.net/DNM/whataboutthesusan.htm.*

29. Passero, "Sue Hendrickson," p. 2.

30. Frankel, "Bone Collector," p. 2.

31. Hendrickson, *Hunt for the Past*, p. 10.

32. Frankel, "Bone Collector," p. 2.

33. Ibid.

34. Hendrickson, *Hunt for the Past*, p. 11.

35. Frankel, "Bone Collector," p. 2.

36. Rachel Louise Snyder, "A tale of two Sues," *Salon*, September 10, 1999, *http://www.salon.com/people/feature/1999/09/10/sue*; memo from Hendrickson to author, September 27, 2003.

37. Quoted in "Sue Hendrickson," *Current Biography Yearbook* (2001), p. 251.

38. Brusatte, "What About the Susan," *http://www.dinodata.net/DNM/whataboutthesusan.htm.*

39. Explorers Journal, Milbry Polk's Interview with Sue Hendrickson.

40. Ask a Dinosaur Expert: Sue Hendrickson, Scholastic Books website, *http://teacher.scholastic.com/activities/dinosaurs/expert/transcript.htm.*

41. Frankel, "Bone Collector," p. 2.

42. Memo from Sue Hendrickson to author, September 27, 2003.

43. Larson, "Story of a Dinosaur," Black Hills Institute of Geological Research website, *http://www.bhigr.com/pages/info/info_sue.htm.*

44. Posted on the Archives of the DINOSAUR Mailing List, Cleveland Museum of Natural History website, *http://www.cmnh.org/dinoarch/2001Mar/msg00197.htm.*

45. Dbit, "Edmontosaurus," *http://www.dinodata.net/Dd/Namelist/TABE/E009.htm.*

46. Larson, "Story of a Dinosaur," Black Hills Institute of Geological Research website, *http://www.bhigr.com/pages/info/info_sue.htm.*

47. Fiffer, *Tyrannosaurus Sue,* p. 41.

48. Malcolm W. Browne, "The Selling of Sue: Tyrannosaur Skeleton May Bring $1 Million, But It's Already Brought Plenty of Trouble," *New York Times,* October 3, 1997.

49. Larson, *Rex Appeal,* p. 121.

50. Hendrickson's edit, p. 49.

51. Browne, "Fetching T. Rex Fossil," November 16, 1996.

52. Browne, "Pity a Tyrannosaur? Sue Had Gout" *New York Times,* May 22, 1997.

53. Browne, "The Selling of Sue," October 3, 1997.

54. Ibid.

55. Jonathan Karl, "Scientists growling over T. Rex auction," CNN.com, *http://www.cnn.com/TECH/9709/03/t.rex/index.html.*

56. Browne, "Tyrannosaur Skeleton Is Sold," October 5, 1997.

57. Fiffer, *Tyrannosaurus Sue,* 211

58. National Geographic, p. 57.

59. National Geographic Dinorama, "A T. rex called Sue," *http://www.nationalgeographic.com/dinorama/sue.html.*

60. "Sue, the biggest T Rex, makes her public debut," CNN.com, May 17, 2000 *http://www.cnn.com/2000/NATURE/05/17/museum.sue.02/.*

61. June Avignone, "3,500 Pounds of Inspiration," Fortune, December 10, 2002, http://www.fortune.com/fortune/proitn/0,15935,397943,00.html.

Notes

62. Joseph B. Verrengia. "T. Rex Named for Maverick Explorer," *Columbia* (Missouri) *Daily Tribune,* May 14, 2000

63. "Franck Goddio," Franck Goddio website, *http://www. underwaterdiscovery.org/english/ icenter/team/franckgoddio.asp.*

64. "Exhibition: San Diego," Franck Goddio website, *http://www. underwaterdiscovery.org/english/ events/exhibitions/madridSanDiego. asp.*

65. "San Diego," *http://storysyn.ngs.org/ yearofpub/1994/sandiego.html.*

66. Memo from Hendrickson to author, September 27, 2003.

67. DiscoverySchool.com, *http://school.discovery.com/ schoolfeatures/featurestories/ cleogame/background.html.*

68. Frankel, "Bone Collector" p. 3.

69. Ibid.

70. Ibid., p. 2.

71. Ibid.

72. Ibid., p. 1.

73. "Bernice Reagon Urges Graduates to Throw Themselves Against Those Things in Life That Should Not Be" *Barnard News,* May 15, 2001, *http//www.barnard.columbia. edu/newnews/news051501com. html.*

Avignone, June. "3,500 Pounds of Inspiration." *Fortune*, December 10, 2002. http://*www.fortune.com/fortune/proitn/0,15935,397943,00.html.*

Barnard News. "Bernice Reagon Urges Graduates to Throw Themselves Against Those Things in Life That Should Not Be," May 15, 2001, *http://www.barnard.columbia.edu/newnews/news051501com.html.*

"Bones to the Highest Bidder." *New York Times*, October 4, 1997, sec. A, p. 14.

Browne, Malcolm W. "Fetching T. Rex Fossil May Fetch $1 Million Plus, Experts Say." *New York Times*, November 16, 1996, sec. 1, p. 9.

————. "Pity a Tyrannosaur? Sue Had Gout." *New York Times*, May 22, 1997, sec. A, p. 16.

————. "The Selling of Sue; Tyrannosaur Skeleton May Bring $1 Million, But It's Already Brought Plenty of Trouble." *New York Times*, October 3, 1997, sec. B, p. 1.

————. "Tyrannosaur Skeleton is Sold to a Museum for $8.36 Million." *New York Times*, October 5, 1997, sec. 1, p. 37.

Brusatte, Steve. "What About the Susan Who Found Sue: A Portrait of Susan Hendrickson," *Paleozoica, http://www.dinodata.net/DNM/ whataboutthesusan.htm.*

"Curse of *T. rex.*" NOVA [television program] transcript for program aired February 25, 1997, *http://www.pbs.org/wgbh/nova/transcripts/ 2408trex.html.*

Frankel, Bruce. "The Bone Collector," *People*, July 24, 2000, p.129ff.

Hendrickson, Sue. *Hunt for the Past: My Life as an Explorer.* New York: Scholastic, 2001.

Hoover, Will. "Archaeologist Travels Far and Wide to Find the Undiscovered." *Honolulu Advertiser*, September 21, 2000. *http://the. honoluluadvertiser.com/2000/Sep/21/921/islandlife.html*

Hoover, Will. "A Fossil Hunter Named Sue." *Honolulu Advertiser*, July 9, 2000. *http://the.honoluluadvertiser.com/2000/Jul/09/islandlife1.html.*

Kane, Julian. "Dinosaur Joins Illustrious Gout-Ridden." *New York Times*, May 29, 1997, sec. A, p. 20.

Larson, Peter, and Kristin Donnan. *Rex Appeal.* Montpelier, Vt.: Invisible Cities Press, 2002.

Passero, Kathy. "Sue Hendrickson: A Real-Life Indiana Jones." *Biography*, November 2000, p. 70ff.

Polk, Milbry, and Mary Tiegreen. *Women of Discovery: A Celebration of Intrepid Women Who Explored the World.* New York: C. Potter, 2001.

Bibliography

Relf, Patricia. *A Dinosaur Named Sue: The Story of the Colossal Fossil: The World's Most Complete T. Rex.* New York: Scholastic, 2000.

Snyder, Rachel Louise. "A Tale of Two Sues." *Salon.* September 10, 1999. *http://www.salon.com/people/feature/1999/09/10/sue.*

Sue Hendrickson. *Current Biography Yearbook* (2001). New York: H.W. Wilson, 2001, pp. 251–253.

Trivedi, Bijal P. "Tiny Tyrant—Fossil May Be Mini T. Rex Cousin." *National Geographic. http://news.nationalgeographic.com/news/2002/08/0809_0208080_TVhadrosaur.htm.*

Verrengia, Joseph B. "T. Rex Named for Maverick Explorer," *Columbia* (Missouri) *Daily Tribune,* May 14, 2000.

Webster, Donovan. "A Dinosaur Named Sue." *National Geographic,* June 1999, pp. 47–59.

Wong, Kate. "Paleontologists Assist *T. rex* Sue's Pathologies." *Scientific American,* October 10, 2001.

Websites

Black Hills Institute of Geological Research Website. "The Story of a Dinosaur Named Sue."
http://www.bhigr.com/pages/info/info_sue.htm.

Cleveland Museum of Natural History Website DINOSAUR Mailing List.
http://www.cmnh.org/dinoarch/1994Sep/msg00095.html.
http://www.cmnh.org/dinoarch/2001Mar/msg00197.htm.

CNN.com. "Scientists growling over T. Rex auction."
http://www.cnn.com/TECH/9709/03/t.rex/index.html
and "Sue, the biggest T Rex, makes her public debut." May 17, 2000.
http://www.cnn.com/2000/NATURE/05/17/museum.sue.02/

Culture.fr Home Page. The First Diving Suits.
http://www.culture.fr/culture/archeosm/archeosom/en/scafan.htm

DinoData Website. Dbit, "Edmontosaurus."
http://www.dinodata.net/Dd/Namelist/TABE/E009.htm

Dominican Republic Factbook.
http://www.cia.gov/cia/publications/factbook/geos/dr.html

Field Museum Website. Sue at the Field Vital Statistics.
http://www.fmnh.org/sue/vital.html

Franck Goddio Website. Exhibition: San Diego.
http://www.underwaterdiscovery.org/english/events/exhibitions/madridSanDiego.asp,
and Franck Goddio.
http://www.underwaterdiscovery.org/english/icenter/team/franckgoddio.asp

History and Archaeology of the Ship. "Spargi."
http://cma.soton.ac.uk/HistShip/shlect43.htm

National Geographic Dinorama. "A T. rex called Sue."
http://www.nationalgeographic.com/dinorama/sue.html

Navydiver.org. Evolution of US Navy Diving.
http://www.navydiver.org/history/default.html

New York Public Library. Cabinet of Curiosities.
http://www.nypl.org/research/chss/events/curiosities.html

Scholastic Books Website. Ask a Dinosaur Expert.
http://teacher.scholastic.com/activities/dinosaurs/expert/transcript.htm

Smithsonian Institution Website. Dinosaur Wars.
http://www.150.si.edu/chap7/dinos.htm

Index

Index

Index

Index

Picture Credits

Contributors

Ann Gaines is a freelance author who lives outside of Gonzales, Texas. She holds master's degrees in American civilization and library science from the University of Texas at Austin. She has written more than fifty nonfiction books for children, including other biographies in Chelsea House's GREAT AMERICAN PRESIDENTS series and WOMEN IN THE ARTS series.

Series consulting editor **Milbry Polk** graduated from Harvard in 1976. An explorer all her life, she has ridden horseback through Pakistan's Northwest Territories, traveled with Bedouin tribesmen in Jordan and Egypt, surveyed Arthurian sites in Wales, and trained for the first Chinese-American canoe expedition. In 1979, supported by the National Geographic Society, Polk led a camel expedition retracing the route of Alexander the Great across Egypt.

Her work as a photojournalist has appeared in numerous magazines, including Time, Fortune, Cosmopolitan and Quest. Currently she is a contributing editor to the *Explorers Journal*. Polk is a Fellow of the Royal Geographic Society and a Fellow of the Explorers Club. She is the also the author of two award-winning books, *Egyptian Mummies* (Dutton Penguin, 1997) and *Women of Discovery* (Clarkson Potter, 2001).

Milbry Polk serves as an advisor to the George Polk Awards for Journalistic Excellence, is on the Council of the New York Hall of Science, serves on the Board of Governors of the National Arts Club, the Children's Shakespeare Theater Board and is the director of Wings World Quest. She lives in Palisades, New York, with her husband and her three daughters. She and her daughters row on the Hudson River.